Wizzy's Bapssang

Easy entertaining at home with recipes
and stories from around the world.

A very special thanks to Ming Tang Evans who donated his time
and photography in the creation of this book.
It wouldn't have been possible without you.

Thank you to everyone who worked on this book:
Joe Buxton for proof reading, the Sky Kong Kong team
and my customers.

I'm honoured you've been a part of this journey.

Wizzy

Contents

Introduction

My wish

Open up the Korean chapter and be charmed by a beautiful photograph before you take a knife to start cooking. Read about Korean history, culture, and of course their fabulous food. Why are Koreans so mad about Kimchi? Understand this and then you will understand Korean food better. Cook wonderful dishes and be able to explain Korean food and history to your family, children and friends.

Open up the British chapter and read an unknown story. If any foreign friend mocks British food, saying it is bad, tell them no, it's good food with a great story. Tell them about 'fish days'. What are fish days? Days made by the Queen. Tell them how brave Elizabeth was. Show them the food and history of Britain.

Mums who have children and full-time jobs are too busy to run the house. However, on special occasions, I hope they can cook new food and be able to explain world histories to their children.

Great food and a bit of history together with fun.

This book covers 13 different countries, their histories and cuisines. It is not a heavy, boring history, but it allows me to explain a little more about the country and their fabulous food. From these histories, I hope you can understand and respect other countries and cultures. I hope you can enjoy going for crazy-coloured food and are not afraid to cook unknown international dishes. It is all about celebrating, entertaining food. I hope you can enjoy it and learn about another country too.

Good food is very simple. Everyone can cook brilliantly as long as you have the following: local, seasonal ingredients, good spices, a bit of artistic imagination, and to gather around you friends and family to eat well with great laughter. With these ingredients, you can cook beautifully.

I think being a chef is one of the best jobs in the world. One of the sexiest jobs. Tasty food makes people happier, so chefs work with passion and enormous energy when cooking. If you are tired of too much work, have a break. Take your passport and knives and go around the world. Sit down and eat well. If I have curiosities, I stop and ask, or learn how to cook a foreign dish. Spend more time in the street market, see the variety of ingredients, and visit local markets. All senses and curiosities suddenly open and you want to know more. Eat well, that is my intention. Street food, small shops and restaurants, I want you to try more.
If I enjoy a meal, I normally send beers to the chef to give thanks and ask about the food. Traveling is all about education and stretching your culinary map, so you are able to cook many different foods.

Curiosity

In the 90's I backpacked across Europe and Asia, visiting many historical places with a lack of knowledge. I had so many questions.

Why do places like the Alhambra palace in Granada have so many Arabic influences? Why was there an Islamic palace in Spain in the first place?

How was Macau (next door to Hong Kong) a Portuguese colony, and when was it founded?

In Goa I was absolutely confused by the architecture. I felt I was somewhere in Europe, due to the many Portuguese influences. I also met Jews in Goa, and Kerala. How were they there?

Malacca, in Malaysia, was a colony of Portugal.

When I travelled to Malaysia, I was impressed by the city Malacca, with its many historical buildings and a mix of European and Asian cultures. A tourist guide explained that the Portuguese, Dutch, British and Japanese all controlled the city at different periods of time. I wondered why so many countries came and went?

That was my initial question, which was left unsolved while I carried on travelling. Only when I became a chef and studied more about international food and history, were my questions answered. The answer was Portugal and it's fabulous spice trade!

They sent sailors and explorers searching for a spice route to India, later conquering it and the surrounding areas. Since the late 15th century, when Vasco da Gama discovered India by sea routes, much of South-East Asia was overtaken by the Portuguese. This included Malacca in 1511, the Spice Islands of Indonesia in 1521 and Macau in 1557.

When I studied food history such as the spice trade through the Silk Road, I discovered quite a lot of information. This route was most beneficial to the Mongols, who used it to gain information to invade other countries. In the process, they ended up connecting Asia to Europe and the Middle East. This study of their history gave me incredible worldwide lessons. I was so fascinated by the spice trade. Through this research, my most interesting discovery was Persian cuisine. How was their cuisine so rich and sophisticated, so well presented, and with such a wise knowledge of handling spices? I was excited to serve new Persian inspired dishes to my customers. But I did not know much. Therefore, it was such a pleasure learning more about their long history and food heritage before I began to cook their cuisine.

A charity cookbook

The Great exhibition – a self-financed endeavour

In 1851 the Great Exhibition was successfully held in Hyde Park in a greenhouse and then the whole thing moved to the Crystal Palace in London, organized by Prince Albert, Queen Victoria's husband. It was a challenge for him to spend less money and still showcase Great Britain's development in engineering, textiles, arts and science. Successfully selling tickets, he and Victoria opened the Victoria & Albert Museum, Science Museum, Imperial College London, the Royal Albert Hall and the Royal College of Art. I was so impressed by how he Developed these projects, and made a huge success of them despite a lack of financing. Even after they made good money they spent that money on the citizens.

Publishing a cookbook

It wasn't my first choice to publish a cookbook. I can cook, but writing is not my strong suit. I came up with the idea to use this book as a charity fundraiser, in order to open a community supermarket with butchers, fishmongers and greengrocers, where both local and international foods could be found. I wanted others to gain access to good food using my skills and knowledge. I was deeply inspired by the Great Exhibition, where instead of spending lots of money, they used their funds to build universities, art museums and music halls. They helped so many people, and still do today. For me, doing charity work by selling a cookbook was an easy and productive way to fundraise, as I did not want to rely on support from the government. I love being independent and making self-supported and fundraised projects. I looked back at myself and what I can do to help people, by using my knowledge and experience. I wanted to introduce good eating habits. That is all I can do.

Once I got the idea I started researching and taking wonderful photographs. My idea was ambitious: to put history and food together in a book. I first chose thirteen countries and regions, to celebrate their food with a story of their nation's hero. This way, people could know and respect other countries. To me, this would be a perfect cookbook. It sounded great but it wasn't easy to work out. After reading how to write a book, I ended up a bit lost. I had ambitions to cover roughly '400 years' of world histories in Europe, the Middle East, Asia, and a bit of America. While covering events spanning the 14th – 17th centuries. I realised how important the 16th century was to world history. If you know what happened during the 16th century, you can easily understand the rest of the world.

Why history?

Personally, many of the projects I imagined and started creating ended up in headaches and problems.

All my concerns were answered in the histories.

Histories that inspired me:

- A Queen selling her own jewellery to support a voyage that led to the discovery of the New World?

- It was the law that you must eat fish three days a week?

- Constantinople was conquered and changed to Istanbul?

Let's start with the Queen who sold her jewellery: Queen Isabella of Spain didn't want to use the nation's treasury to fund Columbus' voyage to India. Instead, she used her own money. But what Columbus discovered on this voyage was not a shortcut to India, but a new land, the New World. He brought back new foods like tomatoes, potatoes, chillies, and tobacco which changed the culinary world forever.

You must eat fish three days a week? It was the law. During the reign of Queen Elizabeth I, she forced the nation to eat fish in order to support the fish industry, as a way to build a strong navy. She ended up winning her war with Spain and paved the way for the British Empire.

Constantinople conquered and changed to Istanbul? Mehmet II was responsible for the fall of Constantinople in 1453. The conflict between the Muslim Ottomans and the Christian Byzantines was another extension of the Crusades. Following the occupation, the Ottoman Empire controlled the spice trade from India which was a disturbing matter to Europeans. This was the reason Queen Isabella sent Columbus to sea, to find a new route and return with spices.

The three of them were smart and brave people, studying non-stop, and fluent in many languages. They all came to power at a very young age, and were insecure, and their countries were very poor. However, all used their energy to build a better country.

The 16th century

Many things occurred during the 16th century. Some topics that were the highlighted for me:
The Renaissance, War, Guns, Protestantism, The New World, Spice trade and Jews.

The Renaissance

After the Black Death killed nearly two thirds of the world's population, people became focused on humanity and reality. Take good care of yourself and be happy in the present. This was the starting point of the Renaissance period from the 14th to 17th century. When the Ottoman Empire took over Constantinople, many of the Christian Italians had to move back to Italy, bringing with them many classic scripts, and their knowledge. It was time for ancient Greek and Roman philosophies and learning to proliferate. The world of art, science, and culture blossomed.

War

Mehmet II never stopped warring, from Turkey to Italy to Bosnia. Wars! So many wars. Europe and the Ottomans fought on land and sea throughout the 16th century. Conflicts involved the Holy Roman Empire, Spain, England, France, and Italy. Over 80 years from 1460 to 1559 the Italian peninsular was in and out of war. Italy was exposed to a vulnerable situation: a civil war, a charming renaissance, and wealthy international trade that tempted the other countries.

Guns

Guns were first introduced in the 14th century but were popularised during the 16th century due to the recurring wars between independent Italian states with the Ottomans and other European countries.
The appearance of the gun was a key change in war, and many Roman Catholic churches were destroyed in their battles.

Protestantism, New forms of Christianity

After many wars in the early 16th century, the Roman Catholics became brutal. Popes were so involved in Italian culture and politics, interrupting hierarchy with greed and corruption, as a result of selling 'indulgences' ('indulgences' were metaphorical tickets to heaven that absolved the receiver from sins committed), in order to rebuild their Churches. Martin Luther, among many others, stood up to this practice and its perceived immorality. This was how the Protestant Reformation started and a new church was born.

The New World

Since the Ottomans took over the spice trade through India, it threatened the European market who could not get to them. By the end of the 15th century, Queen Isabella sent Columbus on a spice route to India, but as he travelled West round the globe, his route to India was interrupted by the New World. A new world of food! After the failure of Columbus, Vasco da Gama (a Portuguese explore) finally joined Europe to India by sea, landing in Goa. Other discoveries of the era included Newfoundland, Canada, in 1497 by John Cabot.

Spain was the first to explore, then Portugal in the 15th century when maritime trade started. In the 16th century they voyaged to Asia and America. In the 17th century England, the Netherlands and France also set out across the sea and conquered more lands.

Jews

After the end of the Reconquista in Spain in 1492, Moors and Jews were expelled. Queen Isabella wanted one country, one religion. Unfortunately, Jews were not welcome in most of Europe either. But Mehmet II welcomed them as long as they paid tax. Jews helped the Ottoman Empire financially, booming the economy through their world-class financial experiences and connections to international trade. This caused a large expansion of the empire. Some Jews moved to the Netherlands and England in the 17th century and did just like with the Ottomans, helped their countries boom economically.

First half of the 16th century - King's League

Henry VIII of England, Francis I of France, Charles V Holy Roman Emperor and King of Spain, and Suleiman the Magnificent were all busy at war. It was a time to change feudalism to strengthen the kingship. All of them were very energetic and clever and keen on war in order to extend their kingdom.

Henry VIII

We all know he married six times and was the father of Elizabeth I and Mary I.

He was charismatic and well-mannered but obsessed with having a male heir to secure the English throne. He had learned many lessons from the 100 Year War between England and France. He didn't sit down and wait for peace, he tried to make it himself. His new church who he was the head of, was created to avoid interference in his power from the Roman Catholic church.

Francis I

A lover of Renaissance arts and artists, he was responsible for bringing Leonardo da Vinci to France, where the Mona Lisa was painted. As much as he loved Italian arts, he developed the French renaissance. For most of his ruling time, he was involved in the Italian Wars and personally rivalled Charles V who had the Holy Roman Empire, ruled Spain, Austria, and a number of smaller possessions neighbouring France. Francis I was constantly threatened. He also allied with Suleiman against Henry VIII and Charles V. He helped the expedition to north America, Canada, Brazil, India, and East Asia.

Charles V

A king of many lands: he ruled over Spain, Italy, and the Holy Roman Empire. In the Americas, he conquered the Aztec and Incan Empires, making his Empire the first on which 'the sun never sets'. He should thank Queen Isabella since the discovery of the New World brought gold, silver, food, materials, and sugar from plantations. He made money through international trade and expanding America, but was also busy making wars with Italy and the Ottomans.

Suleiman the Magnificent

After the courage and success of his hero Mehmet II, Suleiman was able to expand the Ottoman Empire to even more lands. From central Europe to the Mediterranean, and Rhodes Island. He didn't stop there, going to the Red sea and through the Persian Gulf and north Africa. In 1529 the 'Siege of Vienna' echoed across Europe. With this military expansion, the Ottomans were made incredibly wealthy. The 16th century Ottoman Empire was a powerhouse economically, militarily, and politically. Suleiman became a great patron of culture during the 'Golden Age' of the Ottoman empire.

The real winner of the early 16th century was Portugal. They dominated the seas and controlled the East-West trade routes previously owned by the Venetians, Genovese, and Muslim Sultans. Lisbon became a hub of the spice trade. The Portuguese Empire included Brazil, a large part of Africa, and important areas of China, India, Malaysia and Indonesia. From India, they took black pepper and many other spices. From Indonesia, they took nutmeg and cloves. Their routes were kept secret for nearly 100 years, up to the mid-16th century.

In the early 16th century, King Manuel I was the greatest contributor to the Portuguese 'Age of Discovery' with his knowledge of navigation. The wealthy king delighted in exotic pleasures.

Second half of the 16th century – Queen's League

Why Bloody Mary?

A Bloody Mary is a popular cocktail for a hangover cure, and also Queen Mary's nickname. Mary was, unfortunately, intent on killing people in the name of her Catholic religion. Because she married Philip II, who also wanted to return England to a Catholic nation, she killed many Protestants who refused to convert. Without embracing a peaceful policy as head of state, Queen Mary remained Bloody Mary. After five years of reign she shamefully lost Calais, which served as an important port for English goods entering the Continent. She was an unsuccessful queen with her nation collapsing into a disaster.

Mary Queen of Scots

What's wrong with her? Mary was an infant when she inherited the throne of Scotland. She was thrown out of England after Bloody Mary died.

She spent most of her life in France and married the French king, however he died shortly after. In 1560, she returned as a widow to Scotland. She married Lord Darnley and gave birth to a son James, who would inherit the English and Scottish thrones after Elizabeth I. He died under mysterious circumstances in 1567. She mixed with the wrong man after her husband died and married three months after his passing. Their marriage was not accepted, and she ended up imprisoned in England for 19 years for involvement in a conspiracy against Elizabeth. Claims were made that Mary wanted the English throne and was plotting to assassinate Elizabeth. She was found guilty of treason and was executed in 1587. Her death upset Catholic countries and Elizabeth had no choice but to go to war with Spain.

Catherine de Medici

A daughter-in law of King Francis I, member of the Medici family, and a niece of Pope Clement VII. Catherine de Medici married King Henry II of France in 1533. Her father-in-law, King Francis made such an effort for her marriage in order to secure the French throne. She must have expected happiness. Her husband was more engaged with his lover and spent most of his time with her. Catherine endured the humiliation patiently. It took many attempts to become pregnant and she ended up having 10 children. She wasn't a powerful figure in the French court until Henry's death in 1559. Following this, her three sons became Kings of France from 1559 to 1589. This was nearly 40 years where she was in the centre of power and politics. Her biggest fear was religious uprising. Her background was Catholic, which was in conflict with Protestants, causing the French Wars of Religion from 1562 to 1598. Apart from the dark side of civil war, she was a great lover of arts and architecture. Starting with her father-in-law, King Francis I, she continued supporting the French Renaissance, introducing great food, forks, ballet and high heels to the nation. French culture was booming.

Elizabeth I

The real winner of the late 16th century was, Queen Elizabeth I of England. From very early in her reign, she managed to settle a religious agreement. No more fighting within the nation. England was so poor at the time as her father, brother and sister had spent too much money. To raise funds for the rebuilding of the nation, she could either raise taxes or establish the first national lottery. The lottery went ahead and though it set a precedent for future lotteries, it did not gain all the coin she needed. She had to find another way. The answer lay in the New World: a new type of international trade.

The Protestant Reformation in the early 16th century spread new ideas all over Europe. It was 'a time of change'. It was an inevitable movement that some Queens understood, and some did not. The result and was obvious.

Love of Bristol

A new start

Yes, I love Bristol! Moving to Bristol was one of the best decisions I ever made. A while ago one of my friends mentioned to me how beautiful the city was. In 2013, I visited Bristol out of the blue, and fell in love with it from first sight. A small but a decently sized place, lovely old and new architecture, centuries old churches and street art with character. Most of all, I found many allotments not far from the city. It was perfect. Since then, I quit my job, moved to Bristol, and opened a restaurant. I called up the council to ask for allotments. It was the first time I started growing vegetables, herbs, and flowers. I took care of them, fighting with weeds and harvesting them to serve to customers. It was such a joy, dealing with raw materials that I had grown and then cooked.

Markets and Shops

Bristol is home to a multitude of cultures, with over 91 different languages spoken. It's an international city with people of many different backgrounds. If you go to Gloucester Road, you can find more British or European fruits and vegetables. Easton has many Arabic, Indian, African and Caribbean products. The City Centre is home to many Asian products, as well as many local butchers, fishmongers and grocery shops selling international, rare meats and fish, and exotic ingredients. It is a haven for cooking if you are interested. I am very appreciative that this city has everything.

Thanks for the four seasons!

I take a bus to work and see the scenery outside change with the seasons. Rain, wind, snow, sun, I see it all. Spring comes with beautiful daffodils, tulips, and forsythias welcoming everyone. In summer, roses and hydrangea sparkle on sunny days, and green, green, green – it's all around. In autumn, falling leaves, a cold wind and the typical English rain, but still some flowers remain in the garden. In winter, a rare snowy day, but most likely rain and wind.

I love the scenery I see every day. It may be funny to ordinary people, but to chefs it's not. We are people who live in darkness, leaving early in the morning, working mostly in the basement, or in a building with no windows to see the outside world and returning home late at night. We can't see much of the real world. We are isolated from it.

When I started this cookbook, I took many photos to work out things such as table settings and arranging many beautiful flowers. I knocked on my neighbour's door to ask for a donation of flowers from their garden for the cookbook. They all surprised me, donating their lovely flowers for the photos. What a wonderful community spirit. For me, life in Bristol is connecting with people and communicating with strangers. British, Asian, Indian, Caribbean, we all talk and become friends, have a cup of coffee or a meal together, talking about food and listening to their stories. It's so nice to hear from them.

England

John, John, John and the fish, fish, fish days

I was interested to find out who was most influential in helping Queen Elizabeth I to shape England's future and who helped her to find the courage that she needed to fight Spain. Spain was, at the time, the world's strongest country. Compared to the relatively small and poor England, I was surprised to learn that the people who inspired her most at this time were all called John!

John Cabot was an Italian navigator and explorer based in Bristol, who had discovered Newfoundland, in Canada, in 1497 while serving under the commission of Elizabeth's grandfather Henry VII. At that time, Bristol was an international port as well as a being major maritime city. After hearing about the discoveries of Columbus in the New World and Vasco da Gama in India, Cabot was eager for new lands of his own to explore. Elizabeth may not have met him personally, but he was an early influencer for the age of discovering new world ideas. She must have seen the fortunes brought back from this expedition.

John Dee was the Queen's advisor, an astrologer and mathematician. He was a man who mixed science and magic. He was interested in the New World as well as in international affairs. He gave the Queen ideas of what England could grow to be. A highly educated man, he was a respected astronomer and a leading expert in navigation and maps, he trained men who would later conduct English voyages of discovery. Dee also possessed one of the largest personal libraries in history and was a central figure during the Renaissance.

John Hawkins was an admiral as well as a privateer and slave trader. An excellent maritime navigator, he was one of the most successful sailors and navel commanders at Queen Elizabeth's disposal and was in charge of revolutionising the navy with a view to designing the faster ships England needed to combat that Spanish Armada. He was also an early promoter of the slave trade and led a voyage to Africa on a mission to sell slaves to the Spanish plantations in America.

Hawkins returned from his mission in 1563 to find England in the grip of a smallpox pandemic that had even reached the Queen. The Queen was thrilled to have him return and with him she embarked on radical national reforms of industry and farming in an effort to rebuild the country.

In the 1560s, he once again set out on a voyage across the Atlantic Ocean, this time as a privateer, as part of the 'Sea Dogs'. They were a military branch authorised by Elizabeth to attack the Spanish fleet in peace time to loot their ships and bring back treasure.

Fish, fish, fish days

One of Elizabeth's most interesting innovations were 'fish days'. Fish days supported fishermen who formed the basis of the English navy, as well as contributing to the repair, and maintenance of coastal ports. Elizabeth's new rule meant that for three days a week (on Wednesday, Friday and Saturday) you had to eat fish, and this was enshrined by law. Disobeying the new law could land the offender in jail.

Wow, how many fish would people eat in a week? Sounds like a good idea for a nation's diet, even if it is by force. I wish this law existed now, to feed the nation and tackle our issue of obesity.

The idea behind this was that the increased sales of fish would encourage men to go to sea and become fishermen, sailors, or privateers. Training people to become sailors in the navy takes a long time, but the early stages of becoming a fisherman can teach a person a lot. In my opinion, it would have been a great way to learn how to survive at sea.

I think that the three Johns must have had a great influence on her. She learned a lot from their experiences and knowledge, which helped her to get an idea of England's future. In 1558, at the age of 26, she became Queen of England. She was young and insecure, and the country had so many problems that needed to be resolved.

Firstly, the religious conflict between the Catholics and Protestants that threatened the peace and stability of the country. Secondly, the financial outlook of the country: England was so poor after the many wars of her father, King Henry VIII, and her siblings had not looked after the economic welfare of the nation. These were the two main issues that she had to resolve before she could begin to expand the kingdom. She established religious tolerance and ended the killing between the two Christian sects. She tried to live simply, cutting off any unnecessary spending, even reducing the number of staff in court. However, it wasn't enough, and she had to find another way, through the use of pirates.

In the 1560s she accumulated information, and then, in the 1570s, she tested the waters by deploying her new privateers (sailors commissioned by the crown to raid Spanish ships on her behalf). She finally began her war with Spain in the 1580s, and later defeated them with the destruction of their Armada.

Elizabeth's reign was a time of discovery as English ships explored and traded the world. Elizabeth made England a great naval power, which laid the foundations for what would later become the British Empire, a force capable of conquering the world.

There is no doubt that she was smart, not only was she able to speak many languages, but she was a brilliant leader and showed talent for being creative and finding unconventional solutions.

16th Century British food

British food at this time was still heavily influenced by Medieval food as many of the ingredients that we are familiar with today, like tomatoes, potatoes and teas, had not been introduced to the country yet. However, sugar was an expensive luxury product, and some staple seasonings like salt and spices were present in English cooking.

Like A Queen

This menu is inspired by Queen Elizabeth's enforcement of fish days, encouraging more British fish on the table.

Pottage soup
Sallet with flowers
Marzipan
Manchet bread
Seafood platter
Pea soup
Salmon gravlax
Cherry tomato and cod
Deconstructed Eton mess

Pottage soup

This is an old medieval soup that has been eaten for many years.

Leftover roast meat is ideal for this soup; simply shred and save for the next day's soup, served with fresh bread.

The Queen loved to eat this soup with bread for breakfast. Elizabeth I preferred to dine in her chamber alone, thinking about work. Maybe thinking about the war.

I used to live in Worcester Park, near Nonsuch Park in London. I went out for a walk one day, personally surprised by this historical place I had visited many times.

The Treaty of Nonsuch, signed in 1585 by Elizabeth I, supported the Dutch rebel's fight against Spanish rule. Philip II of Spain saw it as a declaration of war. Though she hadn't intended to take action, the Queen made alliances with the Ottomans, Persians, and Moroccans, who were enemies of the Spanish, and prepared for war with Spain.

Serves 4

450g cooked or diced beef
1 onion, finely diced
1 celery stick, finely diced
1 carrot, finely diced
1 turnip finely diced
1 leek (white part only) diced
1litre stock
½ cup of rolled oats
1 tsp red wine vinegar
1 thyme
1 rosemary
1 bay leaf
a pinch of salt and pepper
a sprig of parsley for garnish

Heat the oil in a saucepan and cook the onions, carrots, leeks, celery and turnips for 10 minutes, covered with a lid. Add the stock, bay leaf, thyme, rosemary and stir. Then add the rolled oats and the diced meat. Cover and cook for another 20 minutes. Add the vinegar and season with the salt and pepper. Transfer to a serving bowl and garnish with the parsley and serve with the bread.

Sallet with flowers

The word 'Sallet' comes from the French word 'salade', introduced to England in the 14th century. It is a beautiful sounding word. The Tudor style salad is full of herbs and leaves, as well as pickles, dried fruits and nuts, exotic fruits like Seville orange from Spain, and beautiful garden flowers. We dress it with olive oil.

A linen napkin was draped over the left shoulder for cleaning fingers and a knife, spoon or fingers were used as it wasn't until the late 1600s that forks were in common use in England. The 'sallet' would have been served on wooden or metal plates (ceramics were not yet common in England either).

Serves 4

200g spinach leaves

1 baby gem lettuce

½ carrot, peeled and julienne

2 hard-boiled egg, peeled, cut into halves

1 Seville orange, peeled and sliced

5 morning glory radishes, sliced

1 pear, cored, peeled and scooped

a handful of micro leaves

a pack of edible flower

FOR THE DRESSING:

2 tbsp olive oil

1 tbsp balsamic vinegar

a fresh ground salt and pepper

To make a dressing

Mix the olive oil, vinegar, salt and pepper. Add the salad ingredients and toss gently.

Arrange the salad leaves on the plate with the sliced oranges, carrots, pears, radishes and boiled egg. Garnish with flowers, micro leaves and serve.

Marchpane
(Marzipan)

Like modern marzipan, marchpane is made of almonds and sugar paste. Elizabeth I was known to have quite a sweet tooth and she loved sweet confections. At the time, sugar was more expensive than honey because the sugar came from abroad like the exotic spices that made up many of the dishes from that time. Smiling with black teeth showed one's wealth as it meant you could afford sugar.

Serves 8-10

250g ground almonds
2 tbsp rosewater
175g icing sugar
sugared rose petal
a handful of currants
a small bunch of edible flowers
4 figs
1 egg white, whisked
caster sugar for coating

Preheat the oven to 180°C/Gas Mark 4.

Beat the egg white with a fork until it becomes frothy. Pour a layer of caster sugar onto a plate. Using a pastry brush, coat each rose petal with egg white, then put on the plate and cover in sugar. Dry on a wire rack for an hour.

Using a wooden spoon and a mixing bowl, mix the ground almonds, and icing sugar. Add the rose water and mix well until it combines into a smooth dough. Wrap in cling film and chill for an hour.

Slice the dough into a round shape about 1cm thick.

Transfer them to a baking tray lined with baking parchment and bake for about 10–12 minutes until golden. Allow to cool on the tray. Move to a serving plate and arrange the candied rose petals, currants, flowers and figs, to serve.

Manchet bread

This bread was very popular and eaten in Medieval and Tudor Britain.

The recipe appears in 'The good huswifes handmaide for the kitchen' which was published in England in 1594. It is one of the first English cookbooks.

Serves 4 -6

3 cups whole wheat flour
1 tsp active dry yeast
1 tsp salt
1 cup of beer

Dissolve the yeast in the beer and stir in the salt. Leave to rest for around 15 minutes, or until a brown froth starts to form.

Make a well in the flour and pour in the yeast mixture. Knead the dough until it becomes elastic and then form it into a round loaf. Prick with a knife and leave in a warm place until the dough has doubled in size, it will take 1–2 hours depending on temperature. Preheat the oven to 170°C.

Once the dough has proved, pop it into the oven and bake until golden brown. Leave to cool before serving.

Seafood platter

This is a celebration of Elizabeth I's fish days. Instead of a single fish, why not try a seafood platter? An array of British seafood – local and seasonal – all on one plate.

I think it's sad that this rule of eating fish isn't still in place. Britain consumes less fish than any other island nation and many of the fish caught in British waters are sold to Europe. I hope this will change your mind about enjoying seafood!

Serves 3-4

1 lobster
1 Cornish crab
4 prawns
3 scallops
4 oysters
a small bag of mussels
a small bag of clams
2 lemon wedges

FOR THE DIP:

3 tbsp soy sauce
1 tsp chopped spring onion
1 tsp chopped chilli
a pinch of sesame seed

FOR THE GARLIC MAYO:

1 tsp minced garlic
3 tbsp mayo
a sprinkle of chilli powder
1 tbsp brown meat

Bring a large pot with 5 cups of water to the boil, adding 3 tablespoons of salt. Place the lobster, and the crab in the boiling water and cook the lobster for 8 minutes. Remove the lobster and allow the crab to cook for another 3 minutes. Place both in ice cold water to cool, and then drain.

To shuck the oysters

Wrap a tea towel over one hand and use it to hold the oyster tightly. Using an oyster shucking knife in the other hand, place the tip of the shucking knife at the base of the hinge, and twist the knife to prise the hinge open. Slide the knife along the flat side of the shell to release the oyster.

Wash the mussels in plenty of water. Using your fingers, remove the beard by pulling sharply in the direction of the pointed end. Now you must check that they are alive. Do this by giving any open mussels a sharp tap on a hard surface. If they do not close immediately, discard them.

Place a large saucepan on medium-high heat. Throw in the mussels, the clams, the scallops, the tiger prawns with about 100ml of water. Cover with a lid and steam for around 2 minutes until all have opened. Discard any that remain closed. Chill for use later. Once chilled, remove the half shell and place the meat in it.

Keep all the fish and seafood cold until ready to serve.

To assemble the platter

Take a suitable dish that will hold a handful of crushed ice. Fill with the ice and arrange the seafood. Garnish with some lemon wedges and serve with the prepared sauces. If you can find it, some decorative seaweed makes a nice addition to the platter. I'd recommend chatting up your local fishmonger who should be able to source some for you.

Finish this feast with champagne, and sorbet for a truly elegant experience.

English garden pea soup

Fairly green English pea soup is just so great for starters. This is a dish I learned from the French Michelin starred restaurant, Greenhouse, with my own twist. Freshly ground pea soup is refreshing and clean, especially when served with a dash of yogurt.

Serves 4

200g fresh peas or frozen peas, thawed
¼ cup fresh flat-leaf parsley leaves
¼ cup fresh mint leaves
a freshly ground salt and pepper
1 tbsp olive oil
4 thin slices prosciutto
4 tbsp plain yogurt
4 pea pods or stem (optional)

Add the frozen peas and water enough to cover the peas and bring to a boil. Reduce the heat and simmer for 5 minutes then add the parsley, mint and simmer for another 5 minutes. Plunge into iced water. Pass through a sieve, set aside.

Add the peas, parsley, mint with a bit of water into the blender and blitz for 3 minutes until smooth puree, thinning with water if the soup is too thick. Season soup with the salt and pepper and serve cold.

Salmon gravlax with seasonal fruits in a hibiscus reduction

When creating this dish, I was inspired by a trip to India where I smelt hibiscus flowers, enjoying them in combination with the beautiful and colourful fruit. This dish is just so sexy and beautifully executed. I was overjoyed when I found dried hibiscus flowers in an Asian grocery shop in Easton, Bristol. The colours of this dish are a tribute to a hot summer's day in England.

Serves 4

1 kg salmon fillet, skin on
3 tbsp caster sugar
2 tbsp salt
1 pack cooked beetroot, diced and crushed

100g dry hibiscus flower
100ml water
1 tbsp sugar
1 tsp powder gelatine

8 strawberries cut into a halves
1 mango cut into chunks
1 papaya cut into chunks

1 apple segment
1 peach segment
1 star fruit, sliced

Put the salmon fillets, skin-side down on the salt and sugar. Cover with cling film and chill for 3 days. Remove from the cling film and rinse the salmon to remove the residue and pat dry.

Using a mortar, pound the beetroot until it forms a smooth paste. Cover the cured salmon with the beetroot paste and wrap in cling film for 3 hours.

To make the reduction

Add the hibiscus flower, water, sugar, and gelatine to a medium saucepan and whisk well over a medium heat, then reduce to a slow simmer for around 5-10 minutes, stirring frequently until the gelatine is dissolved.

Remove the saucepan from the heat, and pass the sauce through a sieve into a jug. Pour the mixture into serving dishes and place in the fridge until the reduction is fully set. This will take less than 20 minutes.

Slice each fruit for use as garnish.

Return to the salmon and use a very sharp knife to remove the beetroot, and slice the salmon as thinly as possible. Arrange the slices on a plate by curling them in a circle shape alongside the fruits before serving.

Cherry tomato and cod

This is a perfect summer dish with bold and colourful tomatoes paired with fresh British cod. The ultimate goal of this dish is to celebrate British heritage using local ingredients while making good and healthy food. And what better place to start than with summer tomatoes.

Serves 4

4 small cod loins a long stripe size, about 60-80g each
a few cherry tomatoes
2 tbsp olive oil
1 tbsp white wine
a knob of butter
½ sweet corn
4 asparagus, trimmed
salt and pepper to taste
a few edible flowers (optional)

Bring water to the boil and blanch asparagus for 1-2 minutes, plunge into ice water, set aside.

Using a turning knife crosswise bottom of the tomatoes and blanch them about 2-3 minutes until skin starts to peel off, and plunge into ice water, set aside.

Cook the corn for about 10 minutes, remove and set aside. Once cold using a sharp knife slice lengthwise.

Season the cod loins with salt and pepper and set aside. Add 1 tablespoon of olive oil to a frying pan and allow it to heat up for around 2 minutes. Cook for around 10 minutes on a medium heat, stirring occasionally.

Add the butter and the remaining olive oil to another frying pan. Heat up for 2 minutes then add the cod loins to the pan. Cook for around 3 minutes on each side until just turning flaky. Add the wine to the frying pan and cook for an additional 2 minutes.

Serve the cod on a platter and cover with the tomatoes, asparagus and corn. Garnish with the flower.

Deconstructed Eton mess

"Oops! I dropped it."

The legendary story of this dessert started when two pupils dropped the strawberry, meringue and cream pudding at an Eton vs Harrow cricket match in the late 19th century. They scooped up smashed pieces off the floor into bowls and served it. I have made a little, easy version to recreate the dessert without meringue.

Serve 4

12 fresh British strawberries
8 fresh raspberries

FOR THE REDUCTION:

100g sweet British strawberries halved
1 tbsp sugar
1 tbsp vegetable gelatine

FOR THE TOPPING:

100ml double cream

Combine the berries and the sugar in a saucepan over a medium heat and cook for around 5 minutes.

Transfer the berries to the blender and blitz for 3 minutes until smooth. Sieve them and return to the saucepan. Lightly warm them and add the gelatine. Whisk well until it has completely dissolved. Pour into a serving plate for a very thin layer, shake for a bit and put in the fridge to set.

To garnish

Scatter the strawberries and raspberries and add a spoonful of the double cream to splash over them. Serve.

France

France is known as a culinary country. I wonder why? And when did it all start?

In my opinion it started in the 16th century, and was cemented centuries later after the First World War which stimulated haute cuisine, as science and technology combined with culinary arts, fuelled by the enthusiastic chef's creativity.

Catherine de Medici in the 16th Century

Catherine de Medici was a daughter of the Medici family and known as a leader of Italian Renaissance arts, architecture, and writing. But I want to talk about food. French cuisine is characterized by chefs full of pride for the classics and years of training where only the finest candidates become professionals. But sophisticated cuisine, according to many, began during the 16th century. Many of them believed Catherine de Medici was behind this change. Catherine was key in the creation of the French haute cuisine and the use of the fork for the first time. She came to France with her team of cooks, bakers, patisseries, and new ingredients to add flavour to French dishes. These included bechamel sauce, sorbet, ice cream, marmalade, macaroons, mousse, and card al orange.

1920s in Paris

After a long and dreadful First World War, the devastation through Europe gradually changed into hope. The French economy was booming in the 1920s. Paris was the capital of art, music, literature and cinema, many artists came from around the world: Ernest Hemingway, James Joyce, Josephine Baker, Pablo Picasso, and Salvador Dali, to name but a few. Open to new countries and cultures, all were welcome for the joy of a new open-minded life. For women it was the acceptance of not wearing a corset, trying on trousers for the first time, short haircuts, and smoking in public.

Paris was a truly cosmopolitan city expressing freedom and liberty.

People spent their time at cafés, restaurants, and bistros, eating classic French food alongside food from the New World, talking about love, art and philosophy. There were more cars and trams. Electricity was available at home. And places like saloons, theatres, and other night-time venues were plentiful in the city. Many famous places still exist and have now become must-go places for tourists.

Haute cuisine

A melting pot of culture, French cuisine grew in sophistication throughout the 16th century with haute cuisine, emerging in the 17th century. My work in Michelin starred restaurants wasn't easy – it required lots of very hard work and long hours – but I remember those days as my best culinary experiences as I learned so much. More importantly, I could inject my intellectual knowledge and creative mind into the food I made. These practices will always be with me.

How to be a good chef:

- Be responsible for the food your produce
- Be part of a team
- Find inspiration and creativity in everything
- The importance of controlling your time and energy
- Know how to rest

With long hours of work, if you don't rest properly, it is easy to fall sick or suffer tiredness all the time. Remember self-care. Rest and eat well. The menu that I designed for this chapter is built around contemporary and stylish French cuisine, while still respecting classic dishes and their roots.

Go for bold:

Oyster in blue
Tuna tartare falling in love with fruits
Bouillabaisse
Cote de bouef buried in spices
Chocolate mousse

Respecting classic French cuisine:

Onion Soup
Tea smoked duck breast
Cheese platter

Oyster in blue

Oh! This dish has so many great memories. I came across Yves Klein's striking 'monochrome blue' in an Exhibition in Paris in the 90's. I have since seen his work in galleries around the world, from Japan to Bilbao.

I wanted to lift that blue from the canvas and place it on a plate. 'Absolute blue' became a theme in my cooking; a drop of blue ocean where the oysters come from. It was a perfect pairing, enjoyed with international ingredients. Using fabulous blue pea tea is the key to 'absolute blue' – a technique I learnt in Malaysia.

Serves 4

4 fresh oysters, shucked

½ purple sweet potato cut into bite sized chunks and boiled. (keep skin on)

a small wakame, seaweed, soaked in water

1 tbsp hijiki, seaweed soaked in water

100g vermicelli (or other thin Asian noodle)

1 tsp tapioca, soaked in water

10 blue pea teas or blue colouring

1 tbsp gelatine

1 red chilli, chopped diagonally

a bunch of coriander leaves

½ lemon

Cook the purple sweet potato in water on a medium heat until tender and then drain. Set aside.

Place the blue pea teas in a bowl and pour about 1 cup of boiling water, infusing for 30 minutes. Add gelatine to the blue pea teas or the blue food colouring and cook on a medium heat, mixing well, until dissolved. Pass through a sieve into a jar then pour the jar onto serving plates, turning the plates to ensure an even spread. Put in the fridge for 20 minutes to allow it to set.

Bring a pot of water to the boil and blanch the two types of seaweed for around 1-2 minutes, then plunge into cold water, drain, and set aside.

Cook the tapioca for around 5 minutes, then drain. Cook the noodles for 5 minutes, then plunge into cold water, drain and set aside.

Retrieve the chilled plates and place the oysters on them, seasoning with the salt to taste and squeeze over the lemon.

Then add the noodles, the seaweed, and the tapioca.

Garnish with the sliced chilli and coriander leaves.

Tuna tartare falling in love with fruits

This is the most popular starter at Sky Kong Kong. Western cooking meets Eastern ingredients in this beautiful dish. Using a multi-country selection of fruits, this dish is beautiful and simple with lychee and persimmon and a mix of local ingredients.

I highly recommend this dish for home cooking whenever you are looking for something that has a 'wow factor' that doesn't require too much hassle. This is a timeless dish.

Serves 4

100g fresh tuna fillet, trimmed and diced

1 tbsp grated ginger

1 tsp shichimi (Japanese spice mix)

1 tbsp mayonnaise

1 tsp soy sauce

freshly ground salt and black pepper

1 tbsp Gochujang (Korean chilli paste for garnish)

FOR THE GARNISH:

a couple of green grapes cut into halves

1 fig, cut into quarters

a few spinach leaves

1 small pear, cored, peeled, and cut julienne

4 lychees peeled skin, remain skin on

¼ mango, skinned cut into bite sized chunks

½ persimmon, skinned and cut into bite sized chunks

a bunch of asparagus, trimmed, blanched and cut lengthways

a small bunch of baby broccoli, blanched

1 black garlic, peeled and cut, julienne (optional)

In a bowl, mix together the tuna, freshly ground salt and pepper, soy sauce, grated ginger, the shichimi, and mayo.

To prepare, thinly smear a spoonful of the gochujang on the serving plates, starting from one edge of the plate. Place the tuna and then, on the other side, arrange the persimmon, mango, and grapes. Top with the asparagus, broccoli, spinach, figs, and lychees and then serve.

Bouillabaisse

Marseille's proud seafood dish! Marseille is a port city where they have easy access to fresh seafood from the Mediterranean Sea. If you can find the freshest local fish, you have to try making this delicious recipe!

Serves 3-4

8 prawns

8 clams

100g white fish (cod, haddock, gurnard) cut into bite size chunks

150ml olive oil

1 medium onion, chopped

½ leek, cleaned and sliced

2 carrots, peeled and roughly chopped

½ small fennel bulb, roughly chopped

a pinch crushed dried chillies

100g tomato puree

100ml dry white wine

2 tbsp Pernod

a bouquet garni made from thyme sprigs, bay leaves and parsley stalks

4 garlic cloves, coarsely chopped

½ tsp saffron strands

½ tsp mild curry powder

400g small potatoes, cleaned, peeled, and quartered

salt and freshly ground black pepper

1 tbsp cayenne pepper

a small bunch of dill sprigs, torn

To make a fish stock

Rinse the fish bones and heads thoroughly under cold, running water to wash away any blood still sticking to them. Roughly chop the bones and heads.

Heat the butter in a large saucepan over a medium-high heat until melted. Add the onions, leeks, celery, carrots, and parsley and cook for 3–4 minutes until the vegetables have started to become translucent and softened slightly.

Add the fish bones and heads and fry for 2 minutes then pour in the wine and enough water to cover the fish. Add the bay leaves and black peppercorns, and turn up the heat to bring the liquid to simmer.

Use a skimmer or slotted spoon to remove any foam on the surface.

After 25 minutes, strain the liquid through a fine sieve or even better, through a piece of muslin. The stock is now ready to use.

To make the bouillabaisse, crumble the saffron into the wine in a small bowl. Heat a large pan over a medium-high heat, and add 2 tablespoons of olive oil and cook the celery, onion, and fennel for around 4 minutes, or until it has become translucent but not browned. Add the garlic and tomato purée and fry for 2 minutes, before adding the tomatoes and bouquet garni. Stir well and leave to simmer for 2 minutes. Add the Pernod, white wine, saffron mixture, and the orange zest. Bubble over a low heat until reduced by one-third and then pour in the fish stock. Add the potatoes and reduce the liquid again by one-third before turning down the heat to low.

Pass the soup through a sieve into a clean pan, pressing as much of the liquid through the sieve as you can with the back of a ladle. Season to taste with the salt, pepper and cayenne pepper, and bring back to a simmer.

Heat a saucepan with a drizzle of oil and sauté the garlic with dried chilli until it changes colour, then pour in the white wine and add the shellfish and fish. Cover and cook for around 3-5 minutes.

Carefully place the potatoes, fish, and shellfish onto a warmed serving plate and ladle over a small amount of the soup to serve.

Cote de boeuf buried in spices

This is a French classic. The beef ribeye steak will be loved by any meat lover.

Open up your cupboard and take out all the spices you have for the garnish. Use dried flowers and fresh herbs for a burst of colour.

This is a beautiful recipe that will show your guests that you're giving them the special treatment.

Serves 2-4

1kg trimmed côte de bœuf (bone-in ribeye)

salt and pepper

2 small bunches of thyme, tied with kitchen string

100g salted butter

a splash of olive oil

a bunch of fresh chillies red and green

1 green chilli, chopped

a selection of herbs

Dried fruits and flowers

Selection of spices: tamarind, whole pepper, cinnamon, star anise, coriander seeds, fennel, cardamon, dried chillies, tamarind

Dried fruits

Apricots, figs, prunes, raisins, dates, dried clementine skin (optional)

Dried flowers

Rose buds

Dried herbs

Make sure that your meat is at room temperature before starting. Heat an oven-proof sauté pan to a high temperature on the stove and set the temperature of the oven to 100°C. Add the butter and a dash of olive oil to the sauté pan. Pat the meat dry before placing it carefully in the hot pan. Add one of the bunches of thyme to the pan. You want a nice dark and crusty exterior to the meat, so don't move or turn it until you get it; this should take around 3 minutes per side.

Once both sides are cooked, set the other bunch of thyme on fire, get it really smoking, and add it to the pan and partially cover, leave here for a couple of minutes to get a decent aroma through the meat. Place the meat in the oven, cook for 10 minutes then turn down to 60°C for around 2 hours to get to medium-rare. Remove the meat from the oven and allow it to rest, covered in a warm place for around 20 minutes.

Cover a large plate with the fresh herbs, dried flowers, fruits, and spices. In the centre, place the dish of Côte de boeuf. Slice at the table and serve.

If you can use burnt spices like cinnamon, thyme, and rosemary it creates a great aroma. You must try it

Chocolate mousse

Chocolate mousse is a great way to end a dinner party. Your guests will always have a big smile when they eat this. Creamy, light, and indulgent chocolate is balanced by a deliciously sharp fruit compote.

Serves 6-8

200g milk chocolate, broken into pieces (extra for garnish)

120ml water

3 large eggs

180g unsalted butter, diced

4 tbsp whipped cream

FOR THE FRUITS COMPOTE:

3 cups fresh or frozen fruit (berries), extra berries for garnish

3 tbsp sugar

1 freshly squeezed lemon

Place the fruit and lemon juice in a small saucepan and bring to a medium heat, cover. Once bubbling, reduce the heat and use a wooden spoon to gently stir. Remove from the heat and transfer to ramekins to store in the fridge.

Place the chocolate in a large heatproof bowl set over a pan filled with 120ml of just simmering water, take care to ensure that the bottom of the bowl does not touch the water. Heat gently, stirring until the chocolate is melted and add in the butter, stirring until combined.

Place the eggs into a mixer and whisk for 2-5 minutes until the eggs are smooth and foamy. Start pouring the chocolate mixture into this slowly and mix until all combined.

Spoon the mousse into the ramekins over the fruit mixture and return them to the fridge to chill for a further 30 minutes. Serve with a spoonful of whipped cream, grated chocolate and the berries on top as a garnish

Onion soup

One of the most classic French dishes that dates from Medieval times. Caramelized sweet onions with gooey cheese and crusty bread is irresistible.

Serves 4

60g butter
1kg onion, halved and thinly sliced
4 garlic cloves, finely chopped
2 tsp caster sugar
300ml dry white wine
4 cups beef stock
a bouquet garni of bay leaves, thyme and parsley stalks
4 thick slices French bread
225g gruyere or cheese, coarsely grated
salt and freshly ground black pepper

Heat the butter in a large, heavy-based pan. Add the onions, garlic and sugar and cook over a medium heat, for 20-30 minutes, stirring regularly until the onions are really soft and well caramelized.

Add the wine and leave to simmer rapidly until it has reduced by half.

Add the beef stock and the bouquet garni, cover and leave the soup to simmer for at least another 30 minutes. Then remove and discard the bouquet garni, and season the soup to taste with the salt and pepper.

Meanwhile, preheat the oven to 150°C/Gas Mark 2. Place the slices of bread onto a baking tray and put in the oven for 30 minutes to dry out (note that you don't want them to get brown at all). Then remove the tray and increase the oven temperature to 220°C/Gas Mark 7.

To serve, place one slice of bread for each serving into the bottom of deep ovenproof soup bowls and ladle the soup on top, making sure the onions and stock are distributed evenly. Cover the top of the soup thickly with the grated cheese, and place the bowls onto a sturdy baking tray and bake for 30 minutes or until the cheese has turned golden and is bubbling. This soup should be served scalding hot.

Tea smoked duck breast

This is inspired by the classic dish 'Duck Á L'orange', but with a unique twist of my own. Tea smoked with sugar and spices gives extra aromas to this fabulous dish that is sure to surprise your guests at any party.

Serves 4

4 boneless duck breasts, skin on 2 tbsp vegetable oil

FOR THE MARINADE:

½ tsp freshly cracked black pepper
2 tsp fish sauce
1 tbsp soy sauce
1 tsp sesame oil
1 tsp sugar

FOR THE SMOKING AROMATICS:

½ cup rice
½ cup brown sugar
½ cup mixed tea leaves
2 star anise
3 cinnamon bark
1 tbsp cardamom
1 tbsp dry rose

FOR THE GARNISH:

1 tsp sugar
1 tbsp tea leaves
Mixed spice
4 clementines peeled skin on
1 orange, segmented

Marinate the duck breast with all the marinade ingredients. Cover and chill for 30 minutes. Heat oil on a medium heat and sear the duck, skin side down, for 2-3 minutes. Line the base of a wok with 2 sheets of kitchen foil and the smoking aromatics. Place the seared duck breast on a wire rack with skin side up and close with the wok cover.

Smoke the duck for 5-6 minutes then turn the heat off, allow the duck to rest for 10 minutes before thinly slicing and applying garnish to serve.

Cheese platter

An easy and delicious cheese plate is perfect for any get-together. Enjoy with good wine.
Something old
Something new
Something blue
Or
Something stinky
All works well with fruits, nuts and crackers.

Serves 4-6

1 wheel of epoisses
1 heart of neufchâtel
1 log of sainte maure de touraine
1 wedge St. Agur blue cheese
1 wedge mimolette
a handful of dried apricots, dates and figs
a handful of fresh red or green grapes
a small bag of walnuts
a small dollop of fig or black cherry jam (for hard cheese)
1 pomegranate, peeled
1 pack of biscuits

When planning a cheese platter, its important to ensure that you have a selection of cheeses from which your guests can choose.

A good rule of thumb is to choose one soft cheese (like brie), one hard cheese, one goat's cheese and one blue cheese. Then perhaps throw another of your favourites in there for good measure.

Once you have your cheeses selected, it's time to fill in the gaps with some other tasty treats that complement the cheese. Some great options are fresh fruit like red or green grapes, pomegranate, biscuits, dried fruits such as apricots, dates, or figs and then depending on the cheeses you serve, a small dollop of a fig or black cherry jam.

Spain

Thank you, Queen Isabella! Her support of Columbus to discover the New World brought us some fabulously precious, previously unseen food. Can you imagine the world without tomatoes and potatoes? I know I can't! My favourite tomato sauce is made like this:

Sauté sweet onion and garlic in olive oil.

Add a can of San Marzano tomatoes with a spoon of sugar, toasted fennel, oregano, thyme, and spicy Korean chilli paste.

Add a final pinch of salt and pepper.

Add some chopped fresh herbs and grated cheese.

I highly recommend it. It's sour and sweet with a hint of spice. Absolutely delicious.

We should pay respect to the woman behind this amazing discovery.

Isabella I

Queen Isabella I of Castille was born in 1451. Her father died when she was only three and she and her family were left to the care of the new king, her half-brother, Henry. Sadly, Henry IV was not so inclined to look after her and her family and Isabella, her mother and younger brother were all banished to a rural castle. The poverty and living conditions the family faced were so bad at the castle that her mother became mentally ill. Isabella was devoted to her and her family and, despite such hardship, grew up to be a very smart young lady.

In 1469, at the age of 17, she showed her intentions. By her own will (though against her half-brother, the King's, wishes) she made an adventurous marriage to King Ferdinand II of Aragon, for love and a united territory.

In 1474, aged 22, she became Queen of Castille and Leon, but was left with an empty treasury by her half-brother. Her first act as queen was to reform the nation's laws to find a way to reduce the power of the tyrant nobles that threatened stability in the nation.

War was the answer.

The Moors, native to north Africa, invaded the region of Hispania in the year 711 and established states in western Europe under Islamic rule. The period of their power is known as the Reconquista, which lasted until 1492 when Isabella and Ferdinand defeated the last of the Moors in the Granada War. This united the Spanish nation and Isabella began a mass conversion to Christianity, expelling the Moors and Jewish people. Isabella and Ferdinand failed to see the value and potential of these peoples, and the prosperity that could have been added to the new unified kingdom.

1492 was also the year for another large celebration: the departure of Columbus to seek a new passage to the East Indies. Queen Isabella funded his expedition, which resulted in the discovery of the Caribbean islands and the New World, as well as a plethora of new food, spices, and precious metals such as Gold and Silver. Spain entered a golden age of exploration, colonising this new world and later parts of Asia.

By the time of the reign of Isabella's grandson Charles V, and great-grandson Phillip II, Spain had become a powerful nation capable of waging wars across Europe, the Middle East, Asia, and the Americas. These numerous conflicts solidified the reach of Spain, but often resulted in bankruptcies. Isabella gave up her own personal wealth and assets to ensure the success of her country.

I wonder whether she ever thought that the outcome of investing her jewellery to support a Venetian explorer would have had such an impact.

I also wonder if Isabella had any idea that her discovery of the New World would direct the course of history in such a profound way.

Thank you, Queen Isabella!

Like a warrior: fearless! A decision maker who changed the culinary world!

To this day we celebrate the food of the New World!

Tomatoes, chillies, potatoes, and so much more!

A menu that embraces old and new:

Watermelon gazpacho
Seared salmon with seasonal fruits
Tortilla
Paella with Kimchi
Tapas
Santiago cake

Watermelon gazpacho

Irresistibly sweet and savoury, this watermelon gazpacho is a refreshingly chilled soup, perfect for a hot summer's day. It is blended with lots of summer vegetables and fruits a handful of fresh mint to create a clean and incredibly fresh, sweet summer food.

Serve 4-6

2 cup watermelon, seeded, cut into chunk size

1 cup of water

1 red pepper, seeded, chopped

1 tomatoes, blanched, peeled, chopped

a freshly squeezed lemon

a pinch of salt

1 tbsp sugar

FOR THE GARNISH:

⅓ cucumber, cut into chunks

1 clementine, peeled, segment

⅓ grapefruit, peeled, segmented

½ dragon fruit, peeled, segmented

a small sprig of dill

Place the watermelon, red pepper, blanched tomato, and lemon in a bowl and add the water. Keep it in the fridge overnight or at least a few hours to infuse with all the ingredients.

Combine the ingredients in a blender, blitzing until it becomes a smooth puree. Season with the salt and sugar.

Scoop out the gazpacho into a serving bowl and garnish with the fruits and dill. Serve chilled.

Seared salmon with seasonal fruits

For this dish, you sear salmon in hot olive oil, until it is halfway cooked, then season with soy, lemon, garlic, ginger, sesame oil, sesame seeds, and spring onion. Served with seasonal, fresh, sweet fruit, it's the perfect way to enjoy fish and fruit.

I have served it many times at Sky Kong Kong - especially in winter, when many people want light, savoury food that isn't soup. It's a beautiful dish.

Serves 4

400g salmon fillets
1 tbsp lemon juice
a small ginger, peeled, thinly sliced
1 tbsp minced garlic
1 tsp sesame seed
2 tbsp sesame seed oil
8 tbsp olive oil
salt and pepper
3 spring onion sprigs, finely chopped

FOR THE FRUITS:

½ avocado, peeled, sliced
1 clementine, peeled, segment
1 persimmon, peeled, cut into chunky size
½ pear, peeled, cut into chunky size
½ tomato, seeded, thinly sliced
1 sprig parsley, chopped

Cut the fish into paper-thin slices using a very sharp knife.

Arrange the fish slices on a serving plate with the ginger and the garlic smears and chopped spring onion. Drizzle soy sauce and sprinkle the sesame oil, sesame seeds, and lemon juice over the fish and sprinkle with salt and pepper.

Heat the olive oil in a small frying pan until it begins to smoke.

Pour it over the fish, let it sizzle, then arrange the fruit and herbs before serving.

Tortilla

Spanish tortillas are thinly sliced potatoes, onion, and eggs. A Spanish omelette is perfectly dense and extra satisfying, and can be served hot or cold. It's a fantastic dish served as tapas, or with salad, or a spicy seafood dish like 'gambas al ajillo'. You can add grated cheese or sliced Spanish sausage, or add a jar of smoked red pepper. You can create your own way.

When Queen Isabella sent off Columbus and he came back with food from the New World, I wonder how she reacted to all the new ingredients. Most ingredients weren't commonly used until the 17th century, but potatoes would become essential by the late 16th century. It became a staple food and saved many lives from hunger during national disasters, famine, and pandemics. Moreover, it is irresistibly tasty! It is an everyday comfort food for Europeans. Thanks Queen Isabella!

Serves 4

3 large desiree potatoes, peeled, and quartered, cut into ¼ inch slices

1 onion, quartered, thinly sliced

2 tsp salt

25g butter

2 garlic cloves, minced

8 eggs, beaten to blend

FOR THE GARNISH:

a couple of rainbow potatoes

a few chillies

a few tomatoes

4 small cooked potatoes, skin on

To make the blue plate, see page 36

First make a blue pea plate and keep it in the fridge for about 20 minutes.

Place a large non-stick frying pan on a low heat. Cook the onion slowly in the oil and butter until soft but not too brown - about 10 minutes.

Add the potatoes to the pan, then cover and cook for a further 15-20 minutes, stirring occasionally to make sure they fry evenly. When the potatoes are soft and the onion is shiny, add the garlic and stir, pour the beaten eggs into the potato.

Put the lid back on the pan and leave the tortilla to cook gently. After 20 minutes, the base and edges should be golden with the top set and the middle still a little wobbly.

It's now time for flipping the tortilla.

Place the plate over the pan and turn the whole thing over onto the plate. Slide it back into the pan to finish cooking. Once prepared, transfer a wedge of the tortilla onto the blue plate and garnish to serve.

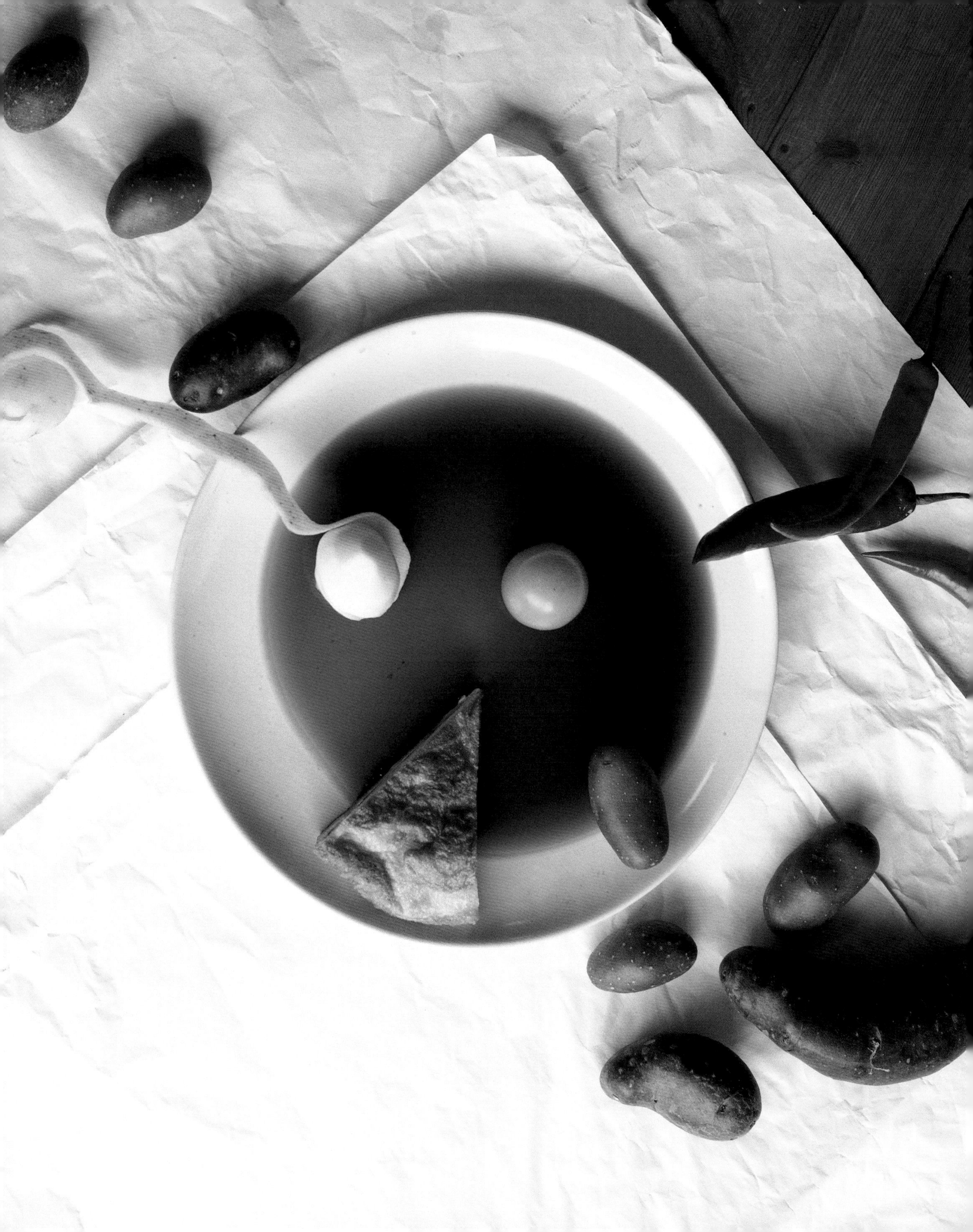

Paella with kimchi

This is Spain's most well-known dish, served with pride and honour in Spanish homes for centuries. Nourishing, vibrant, and so beautiful, it must be served in a big pot and is perfect for sharing, surrounded by family or friends. It is a heritage food.

This recipe is my own twist, inspired by visiting Alhambra palace, which was surrendered to Queen Isabella in 1492 - the same year the New World was discovered and new ingredients began to spread around the world. From West to East, new food flowed. In the same manner, I bring kimchi East to West, fusing cuisine to celebrate global food.

Serves 4

300g paella rice

100g clams, rinsed and scrubbed

100g mussels, rinsed and scrubbed

8 prawns

1 onion, sliced

3 tbsp dry sherry or white wine

400g can chopped tomatoes

1 purple sweet potato

100g kimchi

1 tsp saffron, 1 cup of warm water

50g chorizo sausage, chopped

1 tbsp garlic

1 thyme sprig

900ml chicken stock

1 lemon, ½ for juice, ½ cut into wedges

1 tsp smoked paprika

3 tbsp Sherry

a handful mixed herbs, roughly chopped

salt and pepper

Cover the purple potatoes with water in a pot and bring to the boil for about 15 minutes.

Heat the olive oil in a large frying pan. Add the onion and sauté for 5 minutes before adding the kimchi and sautéing for about 10 minutes. Add the smoked paprika, thyme, rice, and the chorizo stir for 5 minutes then add the sherry and saffron water. Once evaporated, stir in the chopped tomatoes and chicken stock.

Season and cook uncovered for about 15 minutes, stirring now and again, until the rice is almost tender. Add the seafood and cover with a lid. Simmer for 5 minutes or until seafood is cooked through and the rice is tender. Peel and slice the potato and garnish on top of rice. Squeeze the lemon juice, scatter over the herbs and serve with the lemon wedges.

Tapas

Shishito pepper

Serves 4

100g shishito peppers
1 tbsp olive oil
Coarse sea salt (fleur de sel or Maldon)
1 lemon, cut into wedges
a freshly ground pepper

Heat a large heavy-skillet with the olive oil over a medium heat and add the peppers, stirring occasionally until they charred and blistered about 7 minutes.

Return the peppers to the bowl, and toss with the salt and pepper to taste. Serve immediately.

Jamon

Serves 4

4.5kg Jamon
Or 100g sliced Jamon

Slicing ham

You require a long sharp knife for this. Start with the rump half, then the rump end and lastly the shank.

Remove the layer of fat from the top and the sides of the Jamon until the meat is exposed. Trim the fat as you slice. Cut small, very thin slices, including some of the fat which holds much of the flavour. Slice downwards with your free hand behind the knife.

Potato, chorizo and prawn

Serves 4

10 prawns, peeled, veined, roughly chopped
1 potato, peeled and slice
30g chorizo, diced
¼ onion, chopped
1 tsp garlic, minced
a small parsley leaf for garnish
Salt and pepper

Put the potato slices into a pan of cold water. Bring to the boil, simmer for 7 minutes or until cooked. Drain and set aside.

Heat oil in a frying pan, then add the onion and sweat for 5 minutes until soft. Stir through the garlic then add the prawns and chorizo and cook for about 5 minutes. Add the potato slices. Season with the salt and pepper. Garnish with the parsley leaves and serve immediately.

Chorizo stew

Serves 4

400g Spanish chorizo, slice
½ onion, finely chopped
1 can tomatoes, chopped
1 tbsp garlic, minced
1 tsp sugar
salt and pepper

Heat oil in a frying pan, then add the onion and sauté for 5 minutes before adding the chorizo and the garlic. Stir for a few minutes then pour in the tomatoes with the sugar. Leave a lid on, stirring occasionally, and cook for about 20 minutes on a medium heat. Season with the salt and pepper. Serve it warm.

Santiago cake

A traditional cake, dating back to Medieval times. Legend holds that St James's remains were carried by boat from Jerusalem to northern Spain where he was buried on the side of what is now the city of Santiago de Compastela.

This deliciously moist and fragrant honey almond cake will be loved by everyone, and tells the story of Queen Isabella and her devoted religious practice.

Serves 4-8

4 eggs
1 cup of sugar
2 cups of almonds flour
1 lemon zest
½ tsp cinnamon
2 tbsp icing sugar

Preheat the oven to 180°C /Gas Mark 4.

Line a 20cm round cake tin with parchment on the bottom and rub the sides with a little butter. Crack the eggs into a bowl and add the sugar. Whisk the two together until well combined and it starts to become lighter in colour with a bit of air in the mixture. Add the ground almonds, lemon zest and sprinkle cinnamon powder and combine.

Pour the mixture into the prepared cake tin and place in the preheated oven. Bake for approximately 30 minutes until a skewer inserted in the middle comes out clean. Meanwhile, make the cross stencil, if not already prepared, by cutting the shape out of a piece of paper.

Remove the cake from the oven and let it cool for around 10-15minutes on a cooling rack before removing the outer ring. Allow it to cool completely before placing the stencil on top in the middle of the cake and dusting the icing sugar over the top. Carefully remove the stencil without letting the sugar fall on the area you had covered. Slice and serve at room temperature.

Morocco

Morocco

Morocco is full of fabulous, dynamic cities that are marked by the culinary leftovers from Berbers, Arabs, Moors, Jews, and the Spanish, with the fine touch of the French also thrown in. It is the gastronomic door to North Africa. One of Morocco's most recognizable dish is the tagine: a wonderful dish that is infused with many of the key ingredients of the region - spices, couscous, preserved lemons and oranges, dried fruit and nuts, herbs and olives.

The souks of the old Medina are truly Morocco's culinary centre. These are markets that you can visit to buy fresh ingredients. Wandering around the Medina, through its back alleys, one can discover colourful houses, long and narrow streets that reach out across a spread of endless markets selling all sorts of things.

I enjoyed my time in Morocco so much and was enticed by the full aromas of kebabs, kofte, and grilled fish as well as breads and sweet pastries. It made me so hungry!

As a chef, my greatest memory of travelling through Morocco was visiting the souk, fragrant with the scent of orange blossoms and rose petals. It was so exciting to see the wonderful array of spices, dried fruits, olives, and seemingly endless selection of local vegetables alongside the other stores that sold fresh eggs and fish I had never seen before.

After 5pm, I could see the local housewives bringing out their empty baskets to fill them with fresh ingredients for dinner. Local specialties are so popular and so strongly flavoured that there is no room for foreign food. The housewives inspect every ingredient in their hands before they make the purchase, haggling the price and chatting with traders: these women know how to get the best food. This is part of everyday life for them.

The movie Casablanca

I love this movie! It is one of the greatest ever made and describes a rich historical background. An American expatriate, Rick, must choose between his love for a woman and helping her and her husband (a Czech resistance leader) to escape from the Vichy-controlled city of Casablanca and continue the fight against the Nazis.

During the Second World War, Casablanca was a place where people fleeing from the Nazi regime would try to secure transit papers for an onward journey via Lisbon to the ultimate freedom of the United States.

Rick's cafe and theatre, heaving with spies, was the home of refugees. It was a multinational place where exiles lived with locals. Believe it or not, his cafe is still in existence today in Casablanca! Most importantly to me, despite being set in the horrible time of war, this movie has a happy ending and is warm with humanity. It's very soothing.

Like the movie, the themes of love and relationship that are present in Moroccan cooking and can cheer up any friend. Moroccan food can be a food of friendship or a meal of encouragement for a depressed friend, curing their wounded soul.

Moroccan food

Ras-el Hanout is a quintessential blend of spices used in Morocco to marinate meat. The meat is then slow cooked in large tagines with cinnamon, garlic, and dried fruits. Roast peppers, courgettes, tomato sauce and pine nuts are then added for texture. A handful of chopped tomatoes with fresh herbs and a drizzle of lemon juice is added to garnish. For dessert, freshly squeezed orange, watermelon juice, or even a large pomegranate is the perfect way to cool off during the hot midday sun!

A menu has been inspired by the movie Casablanca

Moroccan-style salad
Tuna salad with pistachio crust
Beetroot and garlic yogurt
Chicken tagine
Classic lamb tagine
Moroccan spiced vegetable couscous
Carved watermelon carpaccio

Moroccan-style salad

This wonderfully refreshing salad can be found anywhere in Morocco. It's the perfect small salad - it's like a tonic after the time spent shouting in the crowds and heat in the busy souks. The sweetness of the fruit combined with the sour hint of lemon juice and refreshing herbs make for a slight twist on the North African tradition. It is a beautiful year-round starter that will delight your guests.

Serves 4

100ml orange juice

1 tbsp gelatine powder

2-3 oranges, skin removed and cut into segments

2-3 clementines, skin removed and cut into segments

2 medium sized tomatoes seeded and chopped finely

1 tsp sugar

1 tbsp lemon juice

2 tbsp chopped parsley

freshly ground salt & pepper

4 tbsp pomegranate seeds

a few strands of saffron

8 physalises

Whisk the orange juice and gelatine together in a saucepan over a gentle heat until it begins to bubble. Divide the liquid between the plates and, using a fork, draw circles around the edge of the liquid. Refrigerate until set.

Using a sharp knife, carefully slice off the top and bottom of the orange. Using even, downward strokes, slice the skin away from the flesh and discard. Remove any remaining white pith.
Cut between the membranes to segment the orange, retaining any juices.

Combine the chopped tomato, sugar, and lemon juice in a bowl. Add the chopped parsley and season with salt and pepper.

Take each plate and evenly place the salad mixture and pomegranate seeds around the edge of the circle of the set liquid.

Arrange 3 segments of orange and 3 segments of clementine at even distances amongst the salad mixture. Finally, place two physalises, with their leaves peeled back to reveal the fruit, around the edge of the circle and garnish with 1 or 2 strands of saffron.

Tuna salad with pistachio crust

Fresh tuna coated with a variety of nuts is a sensational combination. You will find such a simple dish unexpectedly delicious. The fresh tuna melts in your mouth and then the coating of nuts provides a surprise. When visiting the fish markets in Morocco, I frequently thought about making this dish using ingredients only found in the market.

Serves 4

2 tuna loins (around 170g each)

2 tbsp pistachios, crushed

2 tbsp black and white sesame seeds

2 tbsp mixed nuts, crushed

1 orange, sliced

½ cucumber, sliced

2 morning radishes, sliced

mixed salad leaves (like rocket or spinach)

2 egg whites, whisked

oil for frying

salt and pepper to season

Use a sharp knife to cut the tuna loin lengthways into 4 pieces. Brush them all over with the oil and season with the salt and pepper to taste.

Heat a pan and add the tuna slices to sear on each side for around 3–4 minutes, the tuna should be rare. Transfer to a plate and keep in the fridge.

Scatter the nuts and sesame seeds onto a plate. Place the egg white in a bowl and brush the tuna with the egg white and roll them evenly in the nut and seed mixture, making sure they are well coated.

Lay a sheet of cling film on a work surface, then place the tuna on it carefully. Wrap it tightly, then return it to the fridge for at least an hour. On a clean chopping board, place and unwrap the tuna. Using a very sharp knife, cut it into 0.5cm slices and place the tuna in the middle of the serving plate and serve with a handful of salad, arrange cucumber, sliced oranges, and sliced radish.

Beetroot and garlic yogurt

Before I discovered this recipe, I found beetroot a bit boring. I am so happy I now understand beetroot's character and I can use the natural colours of the ingredients to create an impact. Freshly cooked red beetroot with creamy yogurt and a hint of garlic is delicious served as a starter or as an accompaniment to meat dishes.

Serves 4

250ml of natural yogurt

1 clove garlic, minced

freshly ground salt and pepper

750g cooked beetroot, cut into wedges

In a bowl, mix yogurt with the minced garlic before adding the salt and pepper to season. Toss the beetroot with the salt and pepper before applying a drizzle of yogurt over the beetroot to serve.

Chicken tagine

This is another Moroccan classic. A tagine using very traditional ingredients: olives, preserved lemons, spices, and herbs. I love the taste of sourness, saltiness, and earthiness all in one dish, with the succulence of the chicken.

Serves 4

1 whole chicken (around 1.5 kg)

water

1 onion, peeled

2 tsp thyme

150g green olives

2 preserved lemons, cut into strips

1 tbsp olive oil

a small bunch of fresh flat leaf parsley, finely chopped

FOR THE MARINADE:

3–4 tbsp olive oil

freshly squeezed juice of 1 lemon

a pinch of saffron threads

a small bunch of fresh coriander, finely chopped

3 garlic cloves, crushed

½ onion, grated

In a bowl, mix all the ingredients for the marinade and rub it all over the inside and outside of the chicken, placing the onion inside. Cover and chill in the refrigerator for 1 hour.

Heat the olive oil and butter in a tagine or heavy-based saucepan and add the chicken, browning it on all sides. Add one cup of the water and bring it to the boil, reduce the heat and cover with a lid. Simmer for around 1 hour, turning the chicken from time to time. Add more water if necessary.

Add the preserved lemons, olives, and thyme. Cover and simmer for 20 minutes.

Season with the salt and pepper before serving with bread or couscous.

Classic lamb tagine

What could be better than slow-cooked lamb with dried fruits? This recipe for aromatic, sweet, succulent, and juicy lamb is a real celebration of the tastes of Morocco.

Serves 4

500g boned shoulder (or leg) of lamb, trimmed and cubed

1–2 tbsp dark honey

3–4 orange rinds

12 stoned prunes, soaked in cold water for 1 hour and drained

6 dried apricots, soaked in cold water for 1 hour and drained

2 cinnamon sticks

a pinch of saffron

1–2 tsp coriander seeds crushed

1 tbsp pine nuts

a thumb sized piece of fresh ginger, peeled and chopped

2–3 garlic cloves, finely chopped

2 red onions, finely chopped

2 tbsp blanched almonds

1–2 tbsp olive oil

a handful of fresh coriander leaves, chopped

sea salt and ground black pepper

Heat the oil in a tagine or a heavy-based casserole dish. Add the almonds and cook, stirring until they turn golden. Next, add the onions and garlic and sauté, stirring in the ginger, saffron, cinnamon sticks, and coriander seeds. Toss the lamb into the dish and sauté for 1–2 minutes, stirring to make sure it is coated in the onions and spices. Pour in enough water to just cover the meat, then bring it to the boil. Reduce the heat and cover with the lid to allow it to simmer for an hour, until the meat is tender. Remove the lid and add the prunes, apricots, orange rinds and pine nuts before closing the lid, allowing it to simmer for another 20 minutes. Stir in the honey, season with the salt and pepper, cover and simmer for a further 10 minutes until the sauce has caramelised and thickened.

Serve with bread or couscous and a sprinkling of fresh coriander.

Moroccan spiced vegetable couscous

Morocco's national dish. No festival or religious ceremony is complete without couscous – it's part of a feast for everyone.

I simply love to cook couscous with plenty of vegetables and herbs. It is delicious on its own, or as an accompaniment to fish and meat.

Serves 4-6

1 red bell pepper, sliced
1 carrot, peeled and diced
¼ butternut squash, diced
1 white onion, thinly sliced
3 shallots, finely chopped
1 red onion, chopped
½ cucumber, diced
a handful of parsley
1½ cups of vegetable stock (or water)
1 cup of couscous
2 tbsp olive oil
15g butter
2 garlic cloves, minced
½ tsp paprika
½ tsp ground coriander
¼ tsp turmeric
½ tsp ground cumin
a pinch of ground cinnamon
a pinch of cayenne pepper
a pinch of salt and pepper

In a pan, bring the stock or water to the boil. Place the couscous into an ovenproof dish and add the liquid. Scatter the butter over the surface and cover with a cling film and allow to stand for 10 minutes to absorb. Bring some salted water to the boil. Add the butternut squash, carrots and courgettes and cook for 5-10 minutes, until tender. Drain and set aside.

Heat the oil in a saucepan and sauté the onion and shallots until soft. Add the sliced bell pepper and spices and season with the salt and pepper.

To finish the couscous, add a drizzle of olive oil and mix with your hands to break up any lumps. Season with the salt and pepper. Add the butternut squash, carrots, and courgettes along with the bell peppers, onions, cucumber, and herbs and serve.

Carved watermelon carpaccio

It's difficult to express how much I enjoyed watermelon while I was in Morocco. This is one of my favourite fruits, especially when in a hot country. Chilled watermelon with honey and sugar, rosewater and infused with mint is the perfect dessert for summer.

Serves 4

½ ripe watermelon
1 tsp sugar
1 tsp honey
1 tbsp rosewater
1 small sprig of mint

Place the fresh watermelon on a clean chopping board, peel the skin and cut it in half. Cut some of the watermelon into 3 x 3cm bite-size cubes and thinly slice the rest with a peeler. Stir the sugar into the rosewater until it has dissolved and pour the scented mixture over the watermelon. Refrigerate for 30 minutes before serving.

Levantine

Levantine food

A star of the eastern Mediterranean region. A meeting point for Europe, Asia, and Africa, the Levantine region was the centre of the world, collecting the best culinary knowledge to create its own cuisine.

A key element of Mediterranean cuisine is the 'perfect meal' - which emphasises fresh fruit and vegetables, plenty of fish, and nuts. This is an idea originating from ancient diets that incorporates the rich religious and geographical diversity of the region.

I was so excited to learn about the ancient diet and of the locations that are rooted this history, eager to learn how each religion influenced the food. The Levant has a painful history, being home to many historic battles, but it has overcome these hardships and adapted, embodying fragments of all the cultures that have passed through it to end up with a truly unique cuisine.

The multi-national region comprises Syria, Lebanon, Palestine, Israel, stretching all the way to Turkey, Jordan, and northern Iran. The region has experienced turmoil throughout the millennium in ancient times it was at one point or another, home to the Phoenicians, Persian Empire, Romans, Byzantine Empire, Christian crusaders, and the Ottoman Empire. It became an international market, as the silk road passed through, as well as being home to the spice trade.

A gateway where Asia meets the Middle East as well as being a door to Europe. The Levant was home to many religions: Christianity, Islam, and Judaism. Their history and cultural background influenced each other's food, and all of these have combined and cohabited to create a colourful culture with a rich history. Through war and peace, love and hate, ultimately, unparalleled food has emerged. It is a passionate cuisine based on family: large feasts are a must.

The three seasons of stunning sunshine that grace the Levant guarantee it incredible agricultural benefits. Its land stretches far and comprises mountains and arid lands bordered by plentiful seas, making it an ideal place to grow incredible vegetables, nuts, grains, as well as fruits and spices that can be dried in the hot sun. Its strategic geographical position within the lucrative Silk Road and Spice Trade allowed for a global marketplace of exotic spices, fabrics and food to develop.

I am a huge fan of meze – it is a classic cooking style where there are plenty of choices of small dishes. I respect the old-style cooking methods and the nutritionally balanced food. That means less red meat, more fish, lots of fruit and vegetables with nuts, seeds, and beans.

A feast-style platter lends itself well to eating together. I remember visiting a house located on the hills with an ocean view surrounded by fruit trees, vegetables, and flowers. The table was set outside under a tree and beside a blazing open fire. This was used to cook charcoal grilled kebab, burnt aubergines for baba ganoush and white fish.

It is a cuisine of ancient ingredients and cooking styles. Lots of olive oil, lemon and orange; dressings of garlic and spices, a splash of yogurt and pomegranate seeds; generous handfuls of herbs and colourful tomatoes; beans and many vegetables straight from the garden. We gathered around the table to share a delightful experience - a perfect midday delight.

Dolma
Fattoush salad
Freekeh salad
Dips: Hummus, Baba ghanoush, Pancar and Hamnera
Fish braised with fennel, tomato and olive sauce
Musakhan

The Mediterranean diet is light. Dishes contain less meat, more fish and vegetables, fruits, nuts, and seeds.

Bake red mullet with cherry tomatoes
Bake stuffed peppers, aubergines, tomatoes in seasoned rice
Artichoke with grill vegetables
Muesli coated prawns with broad beans and green salad
Knafeh

Dolma

This is a wonderful savoury dish that I could eat forever. When I travelled throughout the Middle East, I found vine trees everywhere; growing up the side of somebody's house, by a flat in the city centre, in gardens and palaces, and even outside the shops. The vine leaves are widely used for cooking. Dolma is a seasoned rice dish with spices, herbs and plenty of lemon and pomegranate to create an earthy, scented, and delicious rice.

Serves 4-6

1 jar of preserved grape leaves, about 50 leaves

100g basmati rice, washed and drained

2 tomatoes, seeded and diced

1 tbsp olive oil

1 onion, medium, diced

¼ cup pomegranate

¼ tsp allspice

1 tbsp mint fresh, chopped

1 tbsp parsley fresh, chopped

½ cup of water

1 lemon, sliced

FOR THE SAUCE:

⅔ cup olive oil

1 tsp sugar

4 tbsp lemon juice, freshly squeezed

Preheat the oven to 180°C/Gas Mark 4.

In a bowl, whisk the olive oil, sugar, lemon and a cup of water together and set aside. In a small skillet, sauté the onion and the tomatoes in the olive oil until slightly soft. Reduce to a low heat and add allspice, chopped mint, parsley, and pomegranates. Season with salt and pepper. Add the uncooked rice and stir to combine.

Rinse the grape leaves and pat dry. Spread a layer of vine leaves on the bottom of a large heavy pot or oven proof dish. Place the leaves flat on a large cutting board. Place a heaping teaspoon of the rice mixture near the bottom of the leaf. Fold the bottom of the leaf over the rice, and roll slightly, then fold both sides in and continue rolling to form a cigar shape. Lay all of your dolmas side by side and pour in the sauce.

Cover with foil and cook in the oven at 180°C for around 10 minutes. Then cook on a low heat at 160°C for around 30 minutes or until the leaves are tender.

Allow the dolmas to cool in the pan. Arrange the dolmas on a serving plate, spooning over some of the sauce.

Fattoush salad

Lebanon's most famous salad. Fattoush is a juicy, green salad with crunchy pita bread, an array of herbs, cucumber, tomatoes, and a bright touch of sumac. This fresh salad is highlighted with a load of healthy parsley and squeezed.

Serves 4

2 tomatoes, chopped into chunks

¼ cucumber, seeded and chopped into chunks

1 small head of romaine lettuce, shredded

a handful of mixed herbs (parsley, mint, coriander), roughly chopped

2 pitta breads

3 tbsp olive oil

400g tin of mixed beans, rinsed and drained

salt and pepper

FOR THE DRESSING:

1 tbsp extra virgin olive oil

½ tsp salt

½ tbsp minced garlic

1 tbsp lemon juice

1 tsp sumac

In a large skillet, add 3 tablespoons of oil on medium heat. Add the pita bread and season with the salt and freshly cracked pepper. Fry the pita for 5-7 minutes until the pieces are crispy and golden in colour. (Alternatively, bake the pita bread at 180°C for 5-10 minutes.)

Set the fried bread aside. In a large bowl, add the salad dressing ingredients: the olive oil, garlic, sumac, salt, pepper and lemon juice. Whisk together until the dressing is emulsified and well blended. Add the lettuce, tomatoes, cucumbers, and parsley to the large bowl of dressing and toss to combine. Add the fried pita bread to the salad immediately before serving and gently toss again. Serve chilled.

Freekeh salad

Freekeh is young green grain packed with fibre and is full of nutrients as well as being an excellent source of vegetarian protein. The salad contains plenty of mixed beans, olive oil, vegetables, herbs, grilled apricots, and figs. It's an absolute Mediterranean treat.

Serves 4

1 cup freekeh

2 cups boiling water with a pinch of salt

400g tin mixed beans, rinsed and drained

½ cup of mixed seeds

4 figs, cut into halves

½ red onion, chopped finely

200g cherry tomatoes, quartered

½ cucumber, cut into 1cm pieces

1 cup chopped parsley

½ cup chopped mint

½ cup pomegranate seeds (optional)

1 tbsp lemon

freshly ground pepper

Combine the freekeh, salt, and boiling water in a pot. Cook for 15 minutes. Remove from the heat, strain and cool. If you prefer it a little softer, cook for an additional 5 minutes.

Place the figs and apricots onto the grill pan and grill for 1-2 minutes.

Place the freekeh into a large bowl and add the beans, seeds, onion, cherry tomatoes, cucumber, parsley, mint, and pomegranate seeds. Squeeze over a little extra lemon and season with the salt and freshly ground pepper. Top with the grilled figs and apricots. Serve immediately.

Hummus

A classic and a staple. Hummus is loved in the Mediterranean and throughout the Middle East. It consists of blitzed chickpea, emulsified with olive oil, tahini, garlic, and a heap of cumin. This results in the most creamy, smooth and flavourful dipping sauce, which can be matched with many dishes.

Serves 4-6

200g canned chickpea, rinsed and drained

2 tbsp lemon juice

2 tbsp minced garlic

1 tsp ground cumin

a pinch salt

1 tbsp tahini (sesame seed paste)

4 tbsp water

2 tbsp extra virgin olive oil

FOR THE GARNISH:

a pinch of paprika

a few leaves of parsley

Combine the chickpeas, lemon juice, garlic, cumin, salt, tahini, and water in a food processor, and blend to a creamy purée. Add the lemon juice, garlic, cumin and salt to taste.

Transfer into a bowl.

Drizzle with the extra virgin olive oil and sprinkle with the paprika and parsley, then serve with pita bread.

Baba ghanoush

When I first encountered this dish, I was very shocked, given that it is made with burnt aubergines which gives it that smoky yet creamy taste. It was a great discovery that I enjoyed so much.

Serves 4-6

2 aubergines

2 tbsp garlic, minced

2 tbsp lemon juice, more if necessary

¼ cup tahini

⅓ cup extra-virgin olive oil, plus more for brushing the aubergine

2 tbsp chopped fresh flat-leaf parsley, plus extra for garnish

¾ tsp salt, to taste

½ tsp ground cumin

FOR THE GARNISH:

1 tbsp mix seeds

a small dill leaf

a pinch of smoked paprika

Preheat the oven to 180°C/Gas Mark 4.

On a chopping board, drizzle the aubergine with 2 tablespoons of the olive oil, then toss to coat. Bake in the oven for around 30 minutes or until soft.

Using oven gloves, remove the aubergine from the oven and leave aside to cool. Add the tahini, chilli powder (if using), garlic, cumin, 2 tablespoons the extra virgin olive oil, and the aubergine, discarding the skin. Cut the lemons in half and squeeze in the juice, blitz. Have a taste and add seasoning with the salt and pepper to taste.

Transfer to a bowl and garnish with the mixed seeds, the dill leaf and paprika.

Hamnera - red pepper, pomegranate, walnut

This dish is another surprisingly tasty sauce. The mixture of vegetables, fruits and nuts is great, giving it a sweet, sour, and nutty flavour.

Serves 4-6

4 red peppers

1 large onion or 3 shallots, peeled and cut into chunks

2 cloves garlic, peeled

2 tbsp olive oil

1½ tsp red wine vinegar

4 tbsp pomegranate seeds

4 tbsp roasted and crushed walnuts

salt and pepper

FOR THE GARNISH:

a handful of walnuts

a pinch of parsley

Preheat the oven to 160°C/Gas Mark 3.

Line a baking tray with parchment paper and set aside. Cut the peppers into quarters and remove the seeds. Place on the tray with the onion and garlic. Toss with remaining ingredients. Bake at 160°C for 45-50 minutes, tossing halfway through until the tops of the peppers are starting to brown. Remove from the oven and set aside to cool. Place all ingredients including the oil from the pan into a food processor. Blend for a couple of minutes until totally smooth and transfer into a bowl.

Garnish with the walnuts and parsley to serve.

Pancar - beetroot, yogurt, pistachio dip

Beetroot, yogurt, pistachio - I never imagined to use these 3 items all together, yet the outcome is amazing. It is earthy, and smooth at the same time, as well as having a beautiful colour.

Serves 4-6

400g raw beetroot left whole and unpeeled

2 tbsp olive oil, plus 1 tsp per beetroot, for roasting

salt

6 tbsp plain Turkish or Greek-style yogurt

2 garlic cloves, crushed

2 tbsp chopped pistachio

FOR THE GARNISH:

a pinch of dry rose buds

1 tbsp pomegranate seeds

a pinch of chopped dill leaves

2 garlic cloves, crushed

2 tbsp chopped pistachio

Preheat the oven to 180°C/Gas Mark 4.

Rub each beetroot with 1 tsp oil and sprinkle with a little salt. Wrap them in foil and roast for 1 hour, or until they are soft, and the point of a knife goes in easily. Remove from the oven.

When cool enough to handle, strip off the tough outer skin of the beetroots: use your thumbs to rub it off. Quarter and place in a blender with the olive oil, yogurt, and garlic, add in the pistachio nuts then blitz until smooth. Taste and adjust the seasoning if necessary. Garnish with the dry rose, pomegranate seeds and the dill leaf. Serve with slices of warm flatbread or raw vegetables.

Fish braised with fennel, tomato and olive sauce

This food is representative of Levantine cuisine and culture. The ingredients in this could be easily obtained from your surroundings, either from your own garden or the market.

This is a quick and easy to make Mediterranean fish dish. It uses whole ingredients that are nutritious, and the fish is cooked in a delicious tomato sauce, blended with fennel, garlic, lemon, olives, and herbs. It requires minimal preparation but is incredibly tasty.

Serves 4

4 cod fillets
500ml vegetable stock
1 bay leaf
1 sprig of thyme salt
2 heads of fennel
4 tomatoes, quartered
about 12 olives
a few strands of saffron
1 lemon, halved
3 red dried chillies, broken
1 can tomato sauce
25g unsalted butter
2 bay leaves
2 tbsp minced garlic
1 tbsp sugar
zest of 1 lemon
salt and pepper

Preheat the oven to 180°C/Gas Mark 4.

Trim the fennel and cut off the base, removing the outer layer. Cut each fennel bulb into quarters and squeeze over a little lemon juice.

Place a heavy based saucepan over a medium heat, add the olive oil and butter, and heat until the butter has melted. Add the fennel, season with a little salt, and cook for 10 minutes. Add the tomatoes, garlic, chillies, saffron, and bay leaves, and stir to combine. Then pour in the tomato sauce with the sugar. Cover and cook in the oven for 40 minutes, adding the olives in for the last 5 minutes.

Bring the vegetable stock to a simmer over a medium heat and cook the fish for 10 minutes or until the centre of the fish seems opaque and it flakes easily when prodded with a fork. Do not bring the liquid to a rolling boil, but keep it at a simmer. Taste and adjust the seasoning then scoop the sauce and top with the poached fish. Garnish with the zest of the lemon and some slices of lemon and serve.

Musakhan

This dish is a traditional comfort food and is shared throughout the Levant. Christians, Muslims, and Jews come together to enjoy and share this food, in a harmony of religion and history.

It's more than just roast chicken. It's more robust and is full of flavour with layers of independent character, coming together with sumac and saffron sauteed onions.

Serves 4

1 medium-size whole chicken
1 tsp ground allspice
½ ground cardamom
½ ground cumin
2 tbsp sumac
3 tbsp roasted pine nuts
100g rice, rinsed and drained
salt and pepper

Preheat the oven to 200°C/ Gas Mark 6.

Mix the allspice, cardamom, cumin, sumac, pine nuts in a small bowl to combine. Season the chicken all over with salt in a large bowl. Rub over the spice mix. Place the chicken in a large roasting tray or ovenproof dish lined with non-stick baking paper. Roast the chicken for 30 minutes, then reduce the temperature to 160°C until cooked through and nicely browned onto the top. Cover the chicken with foil and let it rest for another 10 minutes.

Pour in just enough water to cover the rice and bring it to a boil. Reduce the heat and simmer gently until all the water has been absorbed. Turn off the heat, cover the pan, and leave the rice to steam for 10 minutes.

Transfer the chicken to the serving dish and surround it with the rice.

Baked red mullet with cherry tomatoes

A beautifully striped fish that is popular in the Mediterranean. It is simply grilled and cooked with seasonal tomatoes and can be served with plenty of green salad.

Serves 4

4 red mullets, scaled and gutted

2 branches of yellow cherry tomato

2 branches of red cherry tomato

salt and pepper

Heat the oven to 200°C/Gas Mark 6.

Put a roasting tray inside to heat up.

Wash the red mullet, pat dry, and season with the salt and pepper. Add a drizzle of oil to the roasting tray, place in the tomatoes and season with salt and pepper. Next, add the mullet and bake for 8-10 minutes. Serve at once.

Baked stuffed peppers, aubergines, tomatoes in seasoned rice

Upon lifting the pepper's cap, like a hidden parcel, you will be surprised with the gooey cheese underneath. The colourful red pepper is full of umami, thanks to the savoury anchovies, melting cheese and perfectly seasoned rice.

Serves 4

4 red peppers, deseeded
4 medium size tomatoes, deseeded
4 small aubergines, deseeded
150g rice, washed and drained
1 onion, finely chopped
100g anchovies, chopped
100g grated mozzarella or cheddar
2 tbsp minced garlic
2 tbsp tomato puree
150ml vegetable stock
1 tbsp chilli flake
a large handful of chopped parsley and mint
5 tbsp olive oil
salt and pepper

Preheat the oven to 160°C/Gas Mark 3.

Start by preparing the vegetables for stuffing. Cut the tops off the peppers, the aubergines and tomatoes and set the tops aside. In a large pan over medium heat, warm 3 tablespoons of the olive oil and fry the onion and garlic for 3–5 minutes until soft. Add the chopped tomato flesh and tomato purée. Cook for about 10 minutes until soft. Add the rice and 150ml of the vegetable stock, raise to a simmer and cook for 10 minutes, stirring occasionally. Add the anchovies before stirring in the herbs and chilli flakes.

Arrange the vegetable shells on a roasting tin or ovenproof dish and spoon the rice mixture into them. Place the lids on the peppers, the aubergines and the tomatoes and drizzle them all with the remaining olive oil. Pour the remaining stock into the tin, cover with foil and bake for 30 minutes until the vegetables and rice are cooked. Remove the foil and cover with cheese and bake for another 10 minutes until the cheese begins to melt.

Artichoke with grilled vegetables

A green and purple coloured artichoke is definitely one of the wonder vegetables. Raw artichokes have a clean, fresh, earthy, and nutty taste like most vegetables, but once grilled, the flavour becomes more distinct and intensified. When grilled alongside other vegetables, the flavour is enhanced and is smokier, making the vegetables taste better.

When I asked one of my Lebanese friends who has lived in the UK for 40 years what the most memorable food was, he replied: artichokes.

This artichoke dish is for him.

Serves 4

2 large artichokes
a small bunch of asparagus
a few sun-dried tomatoes
1 aubergine, sliced
2 courgettes, sliced
1 lemon
a small bunch of carrots
a small bunch of mixed herbs, roughly chopped
a sprig of rosemary
(for garnish, optional)
1 tbsp of balsamic vinegar (for garnish, optional)
1 tbsp grated charcoal (for garnish, optional)
olive oil
salt and pepper

To prepare the artichokes, use a sharp knife to cut off the top and discard. Cut off the stalk and trim all the way around the base. Cut the artichoke heart in half and with a small paring knife or spoon, remove the spiky, inner choke. Quickly rub the artichoke hearts with the lemon to prevent discolouring.

Squeeze the remaining lemon wedges into a medium-sized bowl. Stir in the olive oil, garlic, mixed herbs, and season with the salt and pepper. Brush the artichokes with a coating of the mixture. Add the aubergine, carrots, asparagus, sun-dried tomatoes and courgette and mix thoroughly. Place them on the preheated grill. Grill the artichokes for 5 to 10 minutes, and the rest of the other Vegetables until lightly charred all over (about 3-4 minutes), basting with the dip and turning frequently until the tips are a little charred. Serve immediately with the remaining dip.

Muesli coated prawns with broad beans and green salad

My main concern whenever I created a menu was how I could incorporate more ingredients to make a dish healthier. I initially came up with the idea to use muesli, to coat prawns and chicken – featured in the Sky Kong Kong menu.

This dish is not a typical Mediterranean food but is inspired by it, using popular ingredients to make everyday food healthier.

Serves 4

8 prawns
oil (to deep fry)
½ cup of muesli
½ cup breadcrumbs
50g flour
3 tbsp ice water
20g podded broad beans
a handful of mixed salad
3 tbsp mixed seeds
a bit of charcoal to grate (optional garnish)
salt and pepper

FOR THE DRESSING:

1 tbsp white wine vinegar
50ml olive oil

Peel the prawn's skin, slice the backs open and remove the intestines, score them and using the back of the knife lightly pat it. Season with the salt and pepper.

Take a bowl and mix the flour with the ice water and whisk it slowly until it becomes a liquid batter. Add the prawns into the batter, coating the entire surface except for the end of the tail. Then, place them in the muesli and roll them over until coated thoroughly. Heat the oil in a deep pan on a high heat, until the temperature reaches 170°C.

Place the prawns one by one in the hot oil and leave them to fry for 2-3 minutes, until they become golden in colour. Remove the prawns using a slotted spoon and place them on a paper towel. Repeat the process with the rest of the prawns.

To make the vinaigrette, whisk the white wine vinegar and olive oil together with some seasoning, then set aside. Boil a pan of water, add the broad beans and boil for 2-3 minutes. Drain and plunge into iced water, then leave to cool a little before removing the skins. Toss the broad beans and mixed salad with the vinaigrette and some seasoning and serve with the prawns, mixed seeds, torn apricots, and a crack of black pepper.

Knafeh

This is a traditional dessert from the Middle East made with thin noodles, or alternatively it can be made with semolina dough and soaked in a scented syrup and is layered with melted cheese.

Serves 4-6

200g knafeh

500g semolina flour

⅓ cup melted ghee

3 tbsp water

2 tbsp ghee or clarified butter, at room temperature, for coating the tin

3 tbsp chopped pistachio nuts

200g shallal cheese

100g akkawi cheese (or mozzarella cheese), shredded

A few dried flowers for garnish (optional)

A few raisins for garnish (optional)

FOR THE SYRUP:

1 cup of granulated sugar

1 cup water

a squeeze of lemon

1 tsp orange blossom water

1 tbsp rose water

Preheat to the oven 180°C/Gas Mark 4.

In a medium saucepan, combine the sugar, water and lemon juice, over a medium high heat. Bring to a boil, then immediately reduce the heat to low and let it simmer for 10 minutes, until the syrup thickens. Stir in the orange blossom and rose water. Set aside.

Using a sharp knife, thinly slice both the shellal and akkawi cheese. Place in separate bowls and cover with lukewarm water to remove the saltiness. Allow the cheese to soak for 2 to 4 hours, changing the water every ½ hour, until the cheese is no longer salty to taste.

Drain both cheeses through a colander, squeezing them with your hands to remove any excess liquid. Crumble both cheeses together with your hands or in a food processor to combine and set aside in the colander to release any excess moisture. If using mozzarella, you can skip this process and use it directly.

Place in a bowl and add the semolina flour, cheese, knafeh, and the ghee. Combine, then add 3 tbsp sugar syrup and 3 tbsp water until well combined and the flour is well coated.

Brush a baking tin with a room temperature ghee, then add the mixture evenly and sprinkle over the bottom of the pan, compressing it with your hands into a compact, even layer. Place in the oven for 20 minutes or until the edge of the crust turns a deep golden brown and the cheese is mostly melted.

Cover the pan and let it rest for a few minutes to allow the cheese to melt all the way through. Sprinkle the reserved 3 tbsp of syrup over the cheese layer to absorb any excess moisture and to prevent the cheese from sticking to the serving platter.

Grease the serving platter with ghee, then invert the knafeh onto it. Pour enough syrup over the knafeh's surface to cover it and spread the syrup with a spatula to even out.

Garnish with chopped pistachio, raisins, and dried flowers. Cut into and serve right away while still warm and the cheese is still gooey.

Ottoman Empire

A challenge to do the impossible

Constantinople, the capital city of the Byzantine Empire, was conquered by the Ottomans in 1453. The commander responsible for this was Sultan Mehmed II, later called 'Fatih' and 'Mehmed the Conqueror'. This ambitious, multi-talented man was only 21 years old at the time, and was believed to have spoken Persian, Arabic, ancient Greek and Italian. He had a vision to expand his empire to Europe and the Middle East.

Before Mehmed arrived, Constantinople had been known for its invincibility. It boasted one of the strongest sets of fortified walls, and behind the wall was a narrow sea called the Golden Horn, which had a set of defensive chains underneath it that could be used to protect the city from unfriendly ships. With these two defence mechanisms Constantinople stayed unconquered for over a thousand years.

Constantinople was renamed Istanbul after Mehmed and his forces conquered the city. The Hagia Sophia church, located on a hill, was converted to Mehmeds's personal mosque. In his palace, he thought about the achievements of his hero, Alexander the Great, and about the future. He studied European art as well as classical literature and histories. He supported the Italian Renaissance artists and had many pieces in his own collection; he founded new palaces, colleges, hospitals, and libraries. Under Mehmed's rule, Istanbul transformed into a totally new city, the seat of a new empire.

From 1453 until he died, Mehmed carried on his ambitious vision of expanding the empire, reforming social systems, and welcoming foreigners of all nationalities. He was open-minded to other religions, with estimated figures showing the population of Istanbul to have been made up of around 60% Muslims, 20% Christians, 10% Jews and others. By the end of the 15th century Istanbul was an international city with a large, multi-cultural population and the centre of the spice trade.

Spice trade

Mehmed would never have imagined that he would inadvertently bring about the discovery of the New World. His control of the spice routes in the Middle East forced the Europeans to go to sea in order to reach India for spices. A new maritime era had begun! War with Europe was becoming increasingly likely as the idea of the Ottoman Turks controlling the routes for spice trading was very disturbing to the European powers at the time. The original spice routes started from the Indian ocean, passing through the Red Sea to reach Egypt before crossing Turkey, the Middle East, and the Mediterranean Sea to reach Europe. This route was firmly in the control of Mehmed and the Europeans had to find another route to India, to the spices.

Ottoman cuisine

Ottoman cooking is derived from a rich culinary tradition with over 500 years of celebrating food.

The imperial Ottoman kitchen prided itself on blending recipes and ingredients as it was a gateway between the East and West and the empire itself conquered many countries. Istanbul has been an international city for many years. It was seen as the door to central Asia and the Middle East, with a controlling influence in the Balkans, Greece, Persia, and North Africa and all these regions influenced its cuisine.

Its culinary heritage grew from many rich sources, using different ingredients taken from different climates and cultures. Ottoman cuisine was truly multicultural.

Even though the great empire is gone, their legacy, culture, historical figures, and food remain in the day-to-day lives of the people today.

The conqueror's menu

Mehmed was responsible for the 'age of discovery' and controlled the spice trade. Nomadic food and spices were his favourite.

Almond soup
Borek
Glorious fish
Stuffed melon
Roast lamb shoulder
Baklava

Almond soup

This is an old recipe found in the Ottoman palace kitchen, dating back to the 15th century when Mehmed II ruled. It was specially prepared for a feast after his sons, Bayezid II and Mustafa were circumcised.

This soup uses almonds to make it rich, creamy, and super comforting. The milk smooth texture, achieved without dairy, can be enjoyed whatever the weather, hot or cold.

Serves 4

100g almonds, blanched and ground
2 tbsp butter
⅓ cup all-purpose flour
1 cup almond milk, warm
¼ cup vegetable stock
a pinch nutmeg
a pinch of salt and pepper

FOR THE GARNISH:
mixed nuts
a few dill leaves
1 fig cut into quarters
1 tbsp mixed seeds
1 tsp olive oil

Melt the butter in a medium-sized pot. Add the flour to the butter, stir, and slowly pour in the milk, stirring constantly. Blend well, using a whisk. Add the almonds, vegetable stock, nutmeg, salt, and pepper. Cook for 20-25 minutes on a low heat, uncovered. Season with the salt and pepper. Ladle the soup into four bowls. Sprinkle with wedges of the fig, nuts, dill and a drizzle of olive oil. Serve immediately.

Borek

Borek are crispy filo pastry parcels made with meat, cheese, spinach, and nuts. While the traditional variant is delicious, I would like to introduce you to this vegetarian version that loses the meat but retains the melting cheese, spinach and pine nuts and is just as tasty.

Serves 4

12 filo sheets (be sure to thaw overnight if using frozen pastry), cut into 10 x 50cm rectangular pieces

⅓ cup olive oil

1 egg white

FOR THE FILLING:

500g fresh baby spinach, washed and dried (I used a salad spinner)

1 onion, peeled, and sliced

1 tbsp olive oil

2 tbsp roasted pine nuts, coarsely chopped

1 pack feta cheese, crumbled

1 egg

FOR THE GARNISH:

a few walnuts and pistachios

1 tbsp pomegranate seeds

a few dried fruits like apricots, figs, prunes, raisins

a few dried flowers

Preheat the oven to 180°C/Gas Mark 4.

Heat the olive oil in a large pan. Add the sliced onion and cook for 3-5 minutes until fragrant. Add the spinach, salt, and pepper and cover with a lid. Cook on a medium heat for around 5 minutes until the spinach wilts. Give it a stir and turn the heat off. Allow to rest for 15 minutes. Once cool, use a mesh strainer to remove the juices. Place the mixture in a bowl with the egg, the pine nuts, and feta cheese and stir it gently until combined.

Prepare a working station to assemble the borek. Spread one filo sheet on the table and brush it gently with olive oil. Fold it in half and brush again with a tiny bit of olive oil. Repeat once.

Now, place about 2 tbsp of the cheese filling on one end of the rectangle. Fold dough over the filling, forming a triangle. Fold triangle over, forming another triangle. Continue folding until you reach the end of the rectangle. Brush the surface of the borek.

Place the borek on a baking sheet and bake for 20 minutes.

Remove from the oven, serve immediately and garnish.

Glorious fish

When I first discovered Mehmet II, I was so fascinated by his story, I wanted to recreate his favourite foods and spices. I visited Turkey and went to his palace, the grand market, museums, and read more about him to find out who he was.

I found a restaurant that served the 16th century food, reviving the cuisine of the Ottoman palace. I spoke to their manager who explained the historical roots of different foods in the Ottoman empire. At the time, fish was extremely popular.

Serves 4

FOR THE FISH:

1 large sea bream or red snapper, scaled, gutted

3 tbsp plain flour

1 tbsp olive oil

½ tsp salt

a handful of prawns

a handful of clams

a handful of mussels

FOR THE GARNISH:

a handful of green and dark grapes

a handful of dried fruits

a handful of mixed nuts

a handful of mixed herbs

4 dried lime (optional)

2 figs, halved

FOR MUSSELS:

20 mussels bearded, cleaned

1 cup short grain rice, washed and drained

1 cup water

1 onion, finely chopped

1 tomato, finely chopped

1 tbsp tomato paste

1 tsp minced garlic

1 tsp sugar

5 tbsp raisins

5 tbsp pine nuts

a pinch of ground cinnamon

a pinch of nutmeg

1 tbsp parsley, finely chopped

1 tbsp dill, finely chopped

⅓ cup olive oil

salt and pepper

1 lemon, cut into wedges

Preheat oven 200°C/ Gas Mark 6.

Heat the oil in a heavy-based saucepan and fry the pine nuts over a medium heat until brown. Add the shallot, garlic, spices and sugar and cook over a medium-low heat for 5 minutes. Stir in the drained rice, the diced tomato, tomato puree paste and raisins. Cook for 2 minutes. Season with the salt and pepper, add 1 cup water and bring to the boil. Turn the heat down and cover with a lid. Cook for 15 minutes, or until the liquid has been absorbed. Transfer the rice to a shallow bowl, stir in the chopped parsley and dill and leave to cool.

Using a small and sharp knife, clasp the mussel and insert the knife between the two shells near the rounded top and cut through where the muscle is attached. Carefully prise the shells open just a little, keeping the mussels in the shells. Take a teaspoon and gently ease an amount of rice into each mussel. Squeeze the shells shut and stack the mussels. Repeat for all the mussels.

Place the mussels on a steaming tray inside a pot. Add 2 cups of water, cover, bring to the boil, then simmer for 20 minutes.

Wash the fish and pat dry, score on both sides with a sharp knife at 2cm intervals, sprinkle with the salt and dust with the flour.

Oil a non-stick frying pan and place the fish over a medium heat for 3 minutes on both sides until the skin is crispy. Remove and place on a baking tray and cook for 10 minutes.

In another pot add 1 tsp of salt, the prawns, clams and pour in ½ cup of water. Cover and bring it to the boil for about 5 minutes until the prawns turn opaque in colour, and the clams open. Set aside.

Remove from the heat and let the mussels cool.

When serving, a large plate or tray works best. Place the fish in the middle, then arrange the mussels, prawns, and clams around it. Finally add the fruits, nuts, herbs, and spices.

Stuffed melon

This special dish dates to the 15th century. Ottoman cooks combined meat, exotic spices and nuts and stuffed them in a melon to release a natural sweetness that was a particular favourite of Sultan Mehmed II.

Serves 4

300g minced beef
1 tbsp minced garlic
50g butter or ghee
1 onion, finely chopped
50g almonds, plus extra for garnish
30g pine nuts
1 tsp allspice
1 tsp cinnamon powder
2 tbsp rice
30g dried fruits and blackcurrants
a pinch of salt and pepper
a few dried fruits and flowers
4 small melons,
a pinch of fresh parsley
a few figs and apricots for garnish

Preheat the oven to 180°C/Gas Mark 4.

Place the meat, garlic, allspice, cinnamon, salt and pepper in a bowl and mix well. Cover and leave to rest for 2 hours. Boil the rice in salted water for 10 minutes. Drain and set aside.

Melt butter in a non-stick pan and brown the onions. Add the almonds and pine nuts and cook until lightly roasted. Now add the meat mixture. When the meat is cooked, add the rice. Mix well and remove from the heat.

Cut off the melon's caps. Scoop out the seeds and stuff them generously with the meat filling. Place 1 tsp butter or ghee in each melon and then some more meat filling and put the caps back on. Line them on a baking tray and brush the outside of the melons with melted butter. Bake for 30 minutes.

When ready, remove the melon caps and sprinkle with the parsley before serving. Garnish with the nuts, seeds, dried flower, fruits and parsley.

Roast lamb shoulder

This is a great hassle-free recipe. Lamb shoulder is more flavoursome than the leg and when seasoned well with the spices, and left to cook low and slow for several hours it will always result in an incredible meaty dish that is succulent and tender.

Serves 4-6

2.5 kg shoulder of lamb
1 tbsp cumin
½ tbsp cinnamon
½ tbsp dried lime powder (optional)
a pinch of salt and pepper

Preheat the oven to 160°C/Gas Mark 3.

Place the lamb shoulder in a roasting tin lined with non-stick baking paper. Put the cumin, cinnamon, and lime powder into a food processor or use a spice grinder and process until finely ground. Drizzle a little oil on to the lamb, rubbing it all over along with the spices and a pinch of salt and black pepper. Roast in the oven for at least 4 hours.

Once cooked, remove from the oven, cover with kitchen foil and leave it to rest for 20 minutes before serving.

Serve with a bowl of couscous.

Baklava

A multi-layered filo pastry, syrup-soaked and infused with cinnamon, cloves and coated with a variety of nuts like walnuts, almonds, and pistachio, served with a touch of lemon juice. It is a delightfully sweet dessert. I used Kafaif noodles as well as filo pastry to get extra crunch.

While I was in Turkey I visited a legendary baklava place, called 'Karakoy Gulluoglu'. The establishment is over 200 years old, and is an important Turkish heritage site. 'Ate heritage'.

Serves 4-6

3 cups of water
3 cups sugar
1 freshly squeezed lemon juice
1 thin strip of lemon peel
1 pack of filo pastry
1 packet kadaif noodles
250g unsalted butter, melted
1 cup of walnuts, coarsely chopped
1 cup of almonds, coarsely chopped
1 cup of pistachio, coarsely chopped
1 tsp cinnamon powder
½ tsp powdered cloves
3 tbsp ground pistachio (for garnish)

Preheat oven 160°C/ Gas Mark 3.

In a large saucepan, over a low heat, mix the water, sugar, lemon juice, and lemon peel, until the sugar dissolves. Simmer for 30 minutes and reduce to a syrup. Allow to cool.

In a mixing bowl, toss in the walnuts, almonds, pistachio, and the spice powders. Meanwhile, divide the filo sheets in half and cut into sheets to fit a pastry tin (ideally about 30 x 20cm). Brush the bottom of the tin with melted butter and cover with a sheet of filo pastry.

Cover this sheet with the nut mix, and then add a layer of kadaif noodles. Repeat this process until you have used all the ingredients. Cover with a thick layer of butter.

Using a sharp knife, cut the pastry layers carefully, making each segment around 10cm long. Bake in the oven for around 15 minutes or until golden brown.

While the baklava is still hot, pour over the cooled syrup and sprinkle with the pistachio before setting aside to cool. Remove from the tray and serve.

Persia

A place where old and new come together to celebrate the nation's favourite dishes. There are some things that spring immediately to mind when I think of Persia: poems, pomegranates, gardens with fountains, caviar, roses, and rosewater.

Honestly, I didn't know much about Persian or Iranian food At first. I wish I had discovered it sooner. From my experience, Persians, Iranians, Iraqis and Kurds of the Gulf are masters of spice. They know what ingredients to use, and how to use them to make great food that stands out amongst the rest.

Whenever I have the chance to meet people from the area, I always ask them what spices to use? Most of the spices they use are homemade. As I can't visit Iran, all of my research comes from the internet, books, videos, and interviews with Iranian natives. I have used this alongside my imagination to create these dishes.

History tells us that the civilization started in Mesopotamia, which is located across modern-day Iran, Iraq, Kuwait, Turkey and Syria. Agricultural communities settled where land was rich and fertile and in time, they grew to be great empires, as evidenced by the Persian Empire.

The ancient Persian Empire was nestled between the Middle East, Africa, and Europe so it was influenced by many foods, cultures and systems.

Persian food

I can't imagine Iranian food without the spices, herbs, nuts, seeds, and its abundance of vegetables. Particularly sour agents such as pomegranates, limes, sour cherries, and sumac. Pomegranate and grape syrups are a highlight of this sour and sweet flavour. Rosewater and saffron are great for cooking rice with. Burnt saffron-infused rice, mixed with nuts, sour berries, and herbs is a particular favourite of mine.

Like many of its surrounding countries, Persian cuisine is replete with stuffed tomatoes, peppers, and kebab dishes. Another Persian dish that I love is slow-cooked, baked chicken rubbed with spices with added pomegranates, oranges, walnuts, vegetables and herbs. It's very impressive and utterly delicious.

Iranian spices

Advieh - cardamon, cumin, cinnamon, dried rose petals, coriander, black pepper, turmeric, dried lime, cloves

Fesenjan - turmeric, cumin, garlic, cinnamon, nutmeg, black pepper with added walnut and pomegranate molasses

Sumac - red sour spices

Grape and cucumber soup
Beetroot and pomegranate soup
Salmon with sumac
Hake with zaatar
Tahchin
Jewel rice
Fesenjoon chicken, walnut, pomegranate stew
Falooleh

Grape and cucumber soup

This tasty cold gazpacho is infused with sweet grapes, refreshing Persian cucumber, and a bunch of herbs. Minimal ingredients are used to create an impressive dish. You can also add yogurt or crunchy nuts.

This is a great dish to have following an indulgent day of eating, serving as a great detox to cleanse your body.

Serves 4

4 cucumbers, peeled, seeded, chopped
1 cup of seedless green grapes
a bunch of herbs (dill, coriander, parsley)
1 cup of water
a freshly squeezed lemon
a pinch of salt
a few sliced cucumber
a few sliced lime
a few sliced grapes
vine leaves (optional for garnish)

In a bowl, add all the ingredients and cover with water and refrigerate overnight.

Combine the cucumbers, grapes, water, and lemon juice in a blender. Blitz until it is a smooth purée. Refrigerate until set. Serve chilled.

Beetroot and pomegranate soup

A beautiful and bold cold soup. The colour is prevalent in the cuisine, bursting with classic Iranian flavours. This hearty, sweet and sour soup highlights pomegranate, a fruit loved by most Iranians. Pomegranate is the symbol of fertility and birth - the gift of God. Yaldā night is an Iranian festival that is usually celebrated with family gatherings. A night where Hafez's poems are read, and pomegranate is consumed. Yaldā is the winter solstice festival and is celebrated on the longest and darkest night of the year.

Serves 4

4 beetroots, cooked, peeled, diced
1 pomegranate
1 cup of water
a freshly squeezed lemon
1 tbsp sugar
1 tsp sumac
1 sprig of dill
1 tbsp pomegranate seeds
1 cooked beetroot, peeled, cut into wedges

Cut the pomegranate in half, turn it upside down and pat using a spatula until all the seeds come out. In a blender, combine the beetroot, pomegranate seeds, water, lemon juice, and sugar to blitz into a smooth puree. Pour into a serving bowl and garnish with the pomegranate seeds, beetroot, and dill.

Salmon with sumac

Salmon is a naturally oily fish, and pairs perfectly with the slightly spicy, sweet, and sour profiles of fragrant sumac. Grilled or roasted salmon - along with a fruity salad - tastes amazing.

Serves 4

4 salmon fillets
2 tomatoes, sliced
4 dried rose petals, finely ground

2 tsp sumac
1 tsp dried lime powder
finely grated rind of an orange

3 tbsp olive oil
a pinch of salt and pepper

lemon slices to garnish
a few dill leaves

Preheat the oven to 180°C/Gas Mark 4.

In a mixing bowl, combine the rose petals, sumac, lime powder, grated orange, add a bit of the olive oil, salt and pepper and mix well. Rub each of the salmon fillets with the spice mix, with the sliced tomatoes and place them on the oven plate. Bake for 10-15 minutes until the fish is cooked. Serve with the lemon wedges.

Hake with zaatar

Zaatar! It's one of the most important spice mixes in the Middle East. It contains various textures and fragrances and has many layers of flavours. It's earthy, nutty, sweet, and sour all in one. The spice is a blend of savoury dried herbs like oregano, thyme, marjoram, coriander, cumin, sesame seeds, salt, and sumac.

Simply steam the fish with the zaatar spice, perfumed with fruits, vegetables, and herbs. It's a great way to enjoy this lovely fish.

Serves 4

4 hake steaks, about 180g each
2 tbsp zaatar spices
¼ onion, peeled, thinly sliced
10 seedless grapes, halved
⅓ cucumber, diced
1 orange, peeled, diced
1 red chilli, finely chopped
1 tomato, seeded, diced
4 morning glory radishes, sliced
1 red pepper, seeded and roughly chopped
a small bunch of coriander
a small bunch of parsley
a freshly squeezed lemon
salt and pepper

FOR THE SAUCE:

1 red pepper, deseeded
1 tbsp lemon juice
1 tsp sugar
100g tomato puree
3 tbsp water

To make the dressing, place the red pepper, tomato puree, sugar, and water into a food processor. Blend until it becomes a puree, add the lemon juice and blitz further. Place the chopped vegetables and the fruits into a large salad bowl and toss with the sugar and lemon juice. Season with the salt and pepper.

Marinate the fish with the olive oil, zaatar spices, salt, and pepper for 30 minutes in the refrigerator. Place the hake in a steamer, bring the water to a boil, and cook for 10 minutes, cooking the fish thoroughly. Remove from the heat.

Put the dressing onto the plate and place the fish in the middle. Place a scoop of the salad on top of the fish. Garnish with the coriander and parsley leaves.

Tahchin

A gorgeous rice dish! Layers of rice are scented with yogurt, saffron, egg, and scattered with beautiful red barberries. Slowly cooking the rice results in the bottom caramelising and burning beautifully to a crisp. The centre is soft and creamy with a hint of tanginess from the barberries. Crunchy on the outside, and fluffy on the inside. It's a dish to die for!

Serves 4

2 cups of long-grain basmati rice, rinsed and soaked in water with 2 tbsp salt for a couple of hours, drained.

3 eggs, yolks

1½ cups of plain yogurt

½ tsp ground saffron, dissolved in 3-4 tablespoons of hot water

a pinch of turmeric

salt to taste

butter or vegetable oil

6 cups of water

FOR THE GARNISH:

1 cup of barberries, plus 1 tbsp for the garnish

1 tbsp almonds

1 tbsp pistachios

Preheat the oven to 160°C/Gas Mark 3.

Bring 6 cups of water to a boil in a large pot on medium-high heat, add the rice and salt and boil for about 8-10 minutes, or until rice grains are soft on the ends and firm in the centre. Drain and pour some cool water over it to wash away the starch and to separate the rice grains. Rinsing with cold water makes the rice fluffier. Set aside to cool down.

Heat oil in a frying pan, add a drop of butter then add the barberries. Toss for around 3 minutes. Set aside.

In a large mixing bowl combine the yogurt, yolks, salt, and saffron. Mix well. Add the rice to the yogurt mixture and stir thoroughly.

In a non-stick pan, add 3 tablespoons of oil and a tablespoon of liquid saffron. Take a non-stick baking dish and spread the vegetable oil to cover. Take half of the rice and press down. Then spread the barberries and pour over the remaining rice. Cover with a lid or wrap with foil. Place in the oven for 30 minutes then reduce to a lower heat and cook for an hour until the bottom is golden brown. When the rice is cooked, stand for 10 minutes. This ensures the crust comes off easier.

Place a plate above the oven dish, flip it upside down and give it a little shake, letting the rice fall from the oven dish, revealing a golden exterior.

Garnish with the nuts and berries. Serve warm.

Jewel rice

Jewel rice is my favourite rice dish. It is so beautifully arranged. Fluffy rice with crunchy nuts and sour fragrant barberries, as well as a super healthy display of pomegranates.

Persians know how to make rice so sexy and tasty, as well as being extremely nutritious.

Serves 4-6

300g basmati rice, washed and drained
3 tbsp pomegranate seeds
1 orange, peel the skin, cut into julienne
3 tbsp barberry berries
3 tbsp pistachio
1 tbsp
a handful of rose buds

Bring 6 cups of water to a boil in a large pot on medium-high heat, add the rice and boil for about 8-10 minutes. Drain the rice and rinse thoroughly under cold running water. Drain the rice and shake it to cool. This process helps get rid of starch, making the rice fluffy.

Add the melted butter to a non-stick pan or heavy pan and add the rice, stirring gently. Wrap with a kitchen towel and cover with a lid, ensuring it is secure and leave for 10 minutes.

In a serving bowl, scoop in the rice and sprinkle with the pomegranates, orange peels, barberries, pistachios, and rose buds.

Fesenjoon chicken walnut pomegranate stew

Fesenjoon is a dish that will pleasantly surprise you. It's rich and succulent, and each bite bursts with flavour. You need to cook it and experience it yourself.

Fesenjoon is one of the most delicious Persian dishes. Biting into the tender, sweet and sour chicken, with tangy pomegranate and the earthy and nutty ground walnut sauce is the perfect experience of the Persian culture, its food and heritage. The ancient recipe takes many hours to complete, however this recipe is a simple and fast version that retains the authentic nature of the food.

Serves 4-6

6-8 chicken thighs, skinless and rinsed

1 large onion, peeled, finely chopped

2 cups shelled walnuts, finely ground in a food processor

1 cup pomegranate molasses

¼ cup sugar, plus more if needed

¼ tsp turmeric

¼ tsp cumin

¼ nutmeg

a pinch of cinnamon

2 cups of water

salt and pepper to season

vegetable oil

Chop the walnuts as finely as possible or pulse them a few times in a food processor. In a large pan add a dash of oil and sauté the ground walnuts until lightly toasted for a minute or two over a medium heat, stirring frequently. Add 2 cups of water, mix well, and cover the pan with a lid and simmer for 30- 40 minutes on low heat.

In a large heavy pot, sauté the onions in 2 tablespoons of oil over a medium heat until golden brown. Add the turmeric and stir well. Place the chicken pieces into the pot and cook until golden brown on all sides, add the salt, pepper, and the rest of other spices.

Add the sugar and pomegranate molasses to the walnut mixture and stir well for 2-3 minutes until it is fully dissolved and the mixture thickens. Pour the pomegranate-walnut mixture into the pot with the chicken and mix well. Add additional water if needed, ensuring the chicken pieces are covered and bring back to a boil. Then lower the heat, cover, and simmer for two hours, stirring thoroughly every 30 minutes to ensure the bottom of the pan doesn't burn. The sauce should be rich and creamy. Taste and add more sugar if you like it sweeter.

Serve sprinkled with the pomegranate seeds and enjoy with rice.

Falooleh

This is an ancient Persian dessert, similar to sorbet. It's made of unusual ingredients such as vermicelli rice noodles, rose water and lime juice. It is an incredibly refreshing dessert that originates from the city of Shiraz.

Serves 4

120g rice vermicelli
1 cup of granulated sugar
⅓ cup lime juice, plus slices and wedges for garnish
2 tbsp rose water
a pinch of salt

Boil the sugar in half a cup of water, add the lime juice and a pinch of salt, and continue stirring until completely dissolved. Remove from the heat and let cool. Place into a freezer until ice crystals begin to form on the edges of the mixture. This will take approximately an hour.

In a medium-sized pot, bring four litres of water to a boil. Add the noodles and cook thoroughly until soft, around 7-8 minutes. Drain and rinse immediately with cold water. Reserve some of the noodles to garnish. Cut the rest of the noodles using scissors into 2.5cm pieces and stir them into the partly frozen syrup mixture. Scrape the granita thoroughly with a fork to prevent icy chunks from forming. The mixture should be light and airy, with fragrant crunchy noodles. Pile the mixture in a glass and serve with the lime slices and wedges and a drizzle of rose water.

South East Asia

Thank you to Nature for the wonderful food and the beautiful landscapes.

If you venture out of the city when you're in South East Asia, you will find that the streets are filled with exotic fruits and flowers. Coconut, papaya, banana, and mango trees are everywhere, often with lemongrass growing underneath them, and passion fruits the size of avocados. You can find unusual and exotic ingredients everywhere. It's a blessing and now I'm living in Bristol, it makes me so envious. There is no doubt that the food in South East Asia is truly magnificent.

Much of this is thanks to its tropical climates that grant it glorious sunshine and plenty of rain that delivers incredible agricultural benefits. With only three seasons in a year, I like to think of it as the land of forever summer. In such weather rice can be harvested three times a year, vegetables all year round, and exotic fruits and herbs can be gathered from fields and mountains. The surrounding seas also produce an abundance of seafood.

Hot and humid weather dehydrates the body, which then requires hot, sweet, and strong flavours to regenerate energy levels. The main forms of seasoning in this region include fish sauce, palm sugar, shrimp paste and kaffir lime leaves. Fruits like mangosteen, honey mango, papaya, passion fruits, coconut, and banana are also used in cooking as well as to make simple but delicious salads.

Every time I go back to Asia, I know that I can find simple yet magnificent food everywhere. Truly genius and genuine street food that humbles me and makes me strive to bring these flavours back to the UK.

All-day eating and night markets

Just after sundown, the city turns on its lights and the food stalls begin to line the streets. Citizens come with home-cooked food to share food made form secret family recipes with the community, and all for a cheap price too! Night markets are often held on Sundays and Mondays, which tend to be less busy days for trading. When it's time, local citizens invade the huge open space hoping to eat well, hold good conversations, and spread the community spirit.

The South East Asian night markets that have left the strongest impression on me are found in Bangkok, Chiang Mai, Phuket, and Penang.

Thailand

Thank you Issan food!

I have eaten a variety of local dishes on my travels in Thailand. Some dishes are internationally famous and some, with their hazy origins, are known only to the local villagers, but when I discovered the food in Issan (Northeast Thailand) I fell in love instantly. The fish dishes were a special delight; many recipes of which I brought home with me to serve in my restaurant, Sky Kong Kong.

They're fairly simple recipes, and that's one of the reasons I love them.

For example: roast a fish, then skin and debone; take its crispy skin and mix it up with vegetables, herbs, and fruits. Season the mix with some fish sauce, lime, sugar, and some lemongrass for scent. Then enjoy.

It's just so perfect! I have tried to adapt my menu to use some of these recipes. One day I served a whole roasted sea bass to my customers. A lot of them loved the fish but I noticed that some of them left the skin. I think it's such a shame as the most nutritious part of the fish is its skin!

Situated in the northeast of Thailand, Issan shares borders with Laos, Vietnam, and Cambodia all along the Mekong River and these places have clearly had an influence on the style and flavours of the food here.

People all over the world love Thai food for its simplicity. It's all about a delicate balance of sour flavours with sweetness and spice. Toss vegetables with lots of herbs, burnt aubergine, and minced pork. Season with a light sauce. It's become my favourite. Som Tam, char-grilled fish, roast chicken with tamarind dips, sausages, sticky rice, are all a highlights of Issan food.

Before we end this chapter, I'd like to introduce you to a long forgotten royal Siamese dish; Kanom Jeen Sao Nam.

Surprisingly light and refreshing, old dishes like this are so hard to find now. A popular dish which was adapted into a variety of recipes by people from all across Thailand and is best for a hot summer afternoon,

The blessing of food

Coming out of the hotel at dawn, you will see unusual scenery. Orange and yellow robed monks carrying bowls line up ceremonially at the markets and houses, where local people fill their bowl with home-cooked food.

This ceremony is called 'Tak Bat'. It's a Buddhist tradition in which food is given in exchange for a blessing, and it takes place in cities and villages across Thailand every day. This humble practice is a real piece of everyday life. It's a beautiful story.

Thailand is an endless paradise of street food! Nothing like any other country I have ever visited. You will find markets, shops, restaurants, and street vendors everywhere, day and night. Delicious food is always waiting around every corner for you to try.

The main seasonings in Thai food are fish sauce, fish paste, palm sugar, chillies and freshly squeezed limes. A spread of vegetables, exotic fruits, and herbs can be found in every dish. Sweet, sour, spicy and salty flavours blend together effortlessly all on one plate.

Celebrating Issan food

Roast snapper with fruits and herbs

Issan food is all about enjoying fish and salad in style. In Thailand, smoked or grilled Catfish would be perfect, but catfish is not popular in the UK. Instead, you can cook any kind of fish this way; for example, I have served sea bass in the Issan style many times in my restaurant. The fish is deboned and shredded, then mixed with chopped vegetables, fruits, herbs some nuts and a squeezed lime. It's a wonderfully simple dish, moist but retaining the incredible smoky fish flavour.

Serves 4

1 whole snapper, or other whitefish (sea bass or sea bream etc)
1 tbsp plain flour for dusting
½ mango peeled, shredded
½ green pepper, shredded
½ red pepper, shredded
½ red onion, shredded
3 tbsp fish sauce
1 fresh lime, squeeze
½ tsp palm sugar
1 tsp chilli powder
2 medium shallots, thinly sliced
3 spring onions, thinly sliced
3 tbsp chopped coriander
3 tbsp chopped mint
2 tbsp chopped dill
Salt and pepper

Preheat oven to 200°C/Gas Mark 6.

To cook the fish, heat a large non- stick frying pan and add a drizzle of oil. Dust the fish with plain flour and sprinkle with a good amount of salt. Once the oil is hot place the fish in the pan, skin side down, and cook for 2 minutes or until the skin is golden and crispy around the edges.

Flip the fish over and cook for a further 2 minutes then take the pan off the heat. Place the fish in the oven for 8 minutes.
Cool down, then debone the fish.

To prepare the salad, whisk the fish sauce and palm sugar until the sugar has dissolved. Add lime juice and chilli powder before tossing through the shallots, spring onion, coriander, mint, dill, mango, red and green pepper. Add the deboned fish with skin and serve.

Smoked aubergine with minced pork and roast rice

This dish is a wonderful combination of smoky burnt aubergine, minced pork and fabulous Thai seasoning with surprising roasted rice. It is nutty, chewy, crunchy, and smoky. This dish is similar to Baba Ghanoush (page 86). The cooking style is evocative of Middle Eastern methods simply adapted with ingredients that are local favourites.

Serves 2-4

2 aubergines
100g minced pork
5 tbsp uncooked sticky rice
1 tbsp chilli flakes
½ tbsp fish sauce
1 lime, freshly juiced
3 shallots, sliced
a few coriander leaves (for garnish)
a fresh red chilli chopped (for garnish)
a pinch of sugar
salt and pepper

Heat a frying pan on a low heat. Toss in the uncooked sticky rice and stir continuously, toast the rice until it turns from white to a golden yellow crust. It will be very fragrant and smell good. Once the rice is toasted, leave it to cool.

Place one aubergine on the gas stove or under a grill and cook until the aubergine skin is burned all over, turning them using kitchen tongs. Once all the skin has blackened, remove from the stove, leave it cool. Repeat this process with the second aubergine.

Fry the pork for around 5-6 minutes until it begins to turn brown. Season with the salt and pepper and take off the heat.

Remove the blackened skin from the aubergines and roughly chop them before placing in a mixing bowl. Add chilli flakes, a pinch of sugar, the fish sauce, a squeeze of lime and the shallots and season with the salt and pepper.

To serve, place the aubergine on a plate and top with the minced pork. Onto this, scatter the toasted rice as well as the coriander and chopped chilli garnish.

Green papaya salad with salted crab

This is an upgraded version of the quintessential Thai classic green papaya salad. Added to it is fermented crab to lend the dish a freshly crisp, pungent and spicy flavour, with a surprisingly sweet finish.

The small crabs traditionally used are found in paddy fields and fermented whole in salted water. Unfortunately, this type of crab is not easy to find, but you can make it with blue swimming crab instead. Don't worry if you can't find it though as Som Tam itself is so delicious. If you have trouble finding green papaya, you can use mango, or mooli (a type of radish) or even kohlrabi instead to achieve a similar flavour.

Serves 2-4

2 salted rice field crabs, roughly broken into pieces (optional) or blue swimming crab

2 cloves of garlic, peeled

5 fresh red chillies

1 tbsp roast peanuts

1 tbsp fish sauce

1 tbsp palm sugar

1 fresh lime, juiced

2 small tomatoes, roughly chopped

a handful of green papaya, shredded (or mango, mooli or kohlrabi)

a handful green beans, trimmed

Peel the papaya using a peeler, or a cheese grater to shave the fruit. Pound the garlic and chillies in a mortar until the garlic is crushed and chillies are reduced to small bits. Add the palm sugar and fish sauce to this mix and then pour the lime juice into the mortar. Mix and pound together to ensure that the palm sugar is fully dissolved.

Add the roasted peanuts and tomatoes to the mortar and pound the mixture lightly to break up the tomatoes. Finally, add in the green beans, crab and a big handful of the green papaya shavings. Mix it all together until the dressing coats all the green papaya and the salad is evenly mixed through.

Serve straight away.

Issan-style chicken

Issan-style chicken is prepared with a honey glaze before cooking over charcoal. The result is an intense flavour, fresh and extra spicy. The key to this dish is in the marinade and charcoal fire, but don't worry if you don't have a charcoal oven, you can achieve similar results using on oven and a grill to finish.

Serves 4

4 boneless chicken breasts, skin on, each cut into 4 pieces

4 boneless chicken thighs, skin on halved

6 garlic cloves, finely chopped

1 tbsp honey

1 tsp sugar

1 tsp salt

1 tsp black peppercorns

1 tbsp fish sauce

a few coriander roots (optional)

FOR THE SAUCE:

4 tbsp skinless raw peanuts

1 small fresh ginger, finely chopped

2 fresh chillies, seeded, finely chopped

1 shallot, finely chopped

1 tbsp soy sauce

1 tbsp palm sugar

3 tbsp tamarind pulp

3 tbsp warm water

For the chicken, using a pestle and mortar, pound the lemongrass with the salt, honey, and sugar to a make a rough paste. Add the garlic and coriander root and continue to pound to a paste. Add the crushed black peppercorns and pound until you have a semi-smooth paste.

Finally, add the fish sauce and mix until well blended. Rub the chicken pieces thoroughly with the paste, cover and allow to marinate in the refrigerator for at least 2 hours. Preheat a ridged cast-iron grill pan until hot, but not too hot.

Place the chicken on the grill pan and barbecue slowly to impart a smoky savoury character and allow the marinade to caramelise. Turn the chicken pieces frequently to prevent them from burning. Cook for 10-15 minutes or until cooked through and caramelised. The chicken is cooked when the juices run clear when the chicken is pierced in the thickest part with a skewer.

For the dressing, dry-roast (without oil) the nuts in a heavy-based pan over a medium heat until golden brown. Shake the pan occasionally to avoid scorching the nuts. Remove from the heat and allow the nuts to cool. Grind the ginger, chillies, and shallots to a paste in a mortar. Add the roasted nuts and continue to crush, then add the palm sugar and work until smooth. Add the remaining dressing ingredients and mix them together. To serve, spoon the roasted nuts and tamarind dressing over the chicken.

Sticky rice

If you want to cook Issan food the right way, I highly recommend mastering this simple dish. It goes perfectly with spicy food and will help to bring down the spice.

Serves 4-6

1 kg sticky rice	**Cover with twice the amount of water**

The night before you want to cook the sticky rice, take your raw rice and place it into a bowl or plastic tub, submerged in water. Allow to soak at room temperature overnight. Take the sticky rice out of the water and wash and rinse a few times. Place it into a bamboo steamer (if you don't have one of these then you can achieve a similar result with any other steamer). Cover the steamer with either a lid or a cloth.

Add water to a pot and bring to a boil. Put the steamer over the pot and steam for 15-20 minutes on a medium heat.

After the rice is cooked take off the lid and taste to test the sticky rice to make sure it's soft and fluffy. Serve when its hot.

Sour soup

Original Tom Sae soup is spareribs in a clear and sour soup. I created this Issan style sour soup, similar to tom yum soup, using king prawns. It's delicious, concentrating on the sour and the spicy.

Serves 4

4 king prawns, cut in half
4 stalks of lemongrass
a small size of galangal
5 fresh red chillies
5 cloves of garlic
2 tomatoes, cut into chunk size
5 kaffir lime leaves
½ onion, sliced
3 tbsp fish sauce
1 fresh lime, juiced
2 tsp sugar
salt and pepper
2 litres water
3 tbsp Thai roasted chilli sauce
100ml evaporated milk

FOR THE GARNISH:

a few fresh mint, torn
1 lemon, sliced
1 garlic, peeled, sliced

Add the onion to a large pan and stir fry until coloured. Then add the galangal and garlic and cook for a couple of minutes until the aroma is released. Add the tomato, chillies, kaffir lime, and the Thai roasted chilli paste until the flavours are released. Add 2 litres of water and bring to the boil until reduced by 2/3. Then add the prawns and milk and simmer for 10 minutes to infuse. Season with the lime juice, fish sauce, sugar, salt, and pepper to taste.

Serve hot and garnish with the lemon, mint, and garlic.

Royal Siamese dish

This is a long forgotten dish from the old Royal Siam, especially served during the Songkran festival celebrated from 13 -15th April. This is a time where Thailand, Cambodia, Myanmar, Laos come together to celebrate their New Year, sharing their delicious food and cleansing water.

It's a smooth and creamy dish of fish cooked in coconut milk served with a fermented soft noodle, with a freshly boiled egg, sliced garlic, and ginger giving it a boost of spice and finished with fresh pineapple to cleanse your palate. It's so refreshing and delicious on a hot summer's day. Songkran coincides with the dry season in April which is the hottest time of the year in South Asia.

Serves 2

200g fillet of firm white fish (you could use sea bass, cod or halibut) cut into bitesize chunks

1 stalk of lemongrass white part only, roughly bruised

a small size of galangal, roughly chopped

2 cups of coconut milk

200g thin rice noodles

¼ pineapple, peeled, shredded

4 eggs, hard-boiled, peeled, cut into half

5 garlic cloves, cut with julienne

2 fresh red chillies, chopped

2 fresh green chillies, chopped

3 tbsp grounded dried shrimps (optional)

salt and pepper

FOR THE DIPS:

3 tbsp fish sauce

1 tbsp sugar

1 tbsp lemon juice

1 tbsp chillies, chopped

Place the fish pieces with the salt and pepper into a food processor, blitz until it becomes a smooth and sticky paste. Use the fish mixture to form little balls the size of a grape. Repeat until all the mixture is used up.

Add 2 cups of coconut milk to a medium pot along with the big chunks of lemongrass and galangal. Bring to the boil then add the fish balls letting it poach until fully cooked (about 3-4 minutes). Keep the coconut milk for later. Cool and set aside.

Fill a large pan with plenty of water and bring to the boil. Add the noodles to the pan and cook around 4-5 minutes until soft. Then plunge into cold water, rinse, and drain.

For the dipping sauce, put the fish sauce, sugar, lemon, and chillies into a mixing bowl and whisk well. Pour into a dipping bowl.

Arrange all the ingredients on a big plate with a small bowl of the cooked rice noodles at the centre. Pour the cooled coconut milk into the small bowl and add the fish balls. Place the dipping sauce on the side, garnish and serve.

Morning glory with clams

This is one of my favourite Thai dishes. When I was in Thailand, I probably had this more than noodle soup. Spicy and sour with fresh clams or cockles and morning glory; I could eat this all day.

Serves 4

500g small clams
1–2 tbsp vegetable oil
2 dry chillies
1 bunch of morning glory
1 tbsp sugar
1 tbsp fish sauce
1 tbsp garlic, minced
3 tbsp water
2 kaffir lime leaves, torn

Soak the clams overnight in salted water.

Wash the morning glory in water, drain and cut into 5cm lengths.

Heat the oil in a wok then add the garlic and chillies. Stir-fry until the garlic is golden then add the fish sauce, sugar, and water. Wait for 1 minute then add the clams along with the morning glory. Once the morning glory has wilted and the clams have opened, turn down the heat. Scatter the torn kaffir lime leaves to serve.

Pomelo, coconut peanut salad

A light Thai lunch dish, consisting of juicy pomelo segments, peanuts and coconut with refreshing vegetables and herbs.

Serves 4

1 lime, pith removed, rind reserved

1 cup of shredded coconut, toasted

½ cup unsalted roasted peanuts, roughly chopped

10 cooked prawns, peeled and chopped

3 red bird's eye chillies, finely chopped

12 betel leaves (or torn lettuce or spinach leaves if you can't find betel leaves)

1 cup pomelo segments, peeled and broken

½ red onion, chopped

2 tbsp fish sauce

1 tbsp tamarind puree

3 tbsp sugar

3cm piece galangal or ginger, cut into 3 slices (or 1tsp ground galangal or ginger powder if you can't find them fresh)

salt and pepper

Place the fish sauce, tamarind puree, and sugar in a mixing bowl and mix until sugar is dissolved. Then add the cooked prawns and season with the salt and pepper. Toss with the remaining ingredients and serve over the betel leaves.

Pad Thai

Craving an authentic Thai street food? This freshly stir-fried rice noodle dish is bursting with flavour, from sweet and tangy, to salty and spicy. Combined with roasted peanut, chillies flakes, and a lime wedge,Pad Thai has more of a story to tell.

This dish was created by a former prime minster back in the 1930s in Thailand. A campaign titled 'build a nation' was set in motion and 'Pad Thai' was promoted across the country. During World War II rice was in shortage so to decrease national dependency on rice they invented a new dish using noodles.

They also wanted to improve the variety of the Thai diet, and a more important message was to promote unity in Thailand, and a sense of national identity across the nation by creating a food that everyone would love.

Serves 4

300g dried flat rice noodle
3 tbsp fish sauce
2 tbsp palm sugar
2 tbsp tamarind water
1 small bunch of Chinese chives cut into 2cm
2 tsp oil
2 shallots, chopped
1 egg
50g firm tofu, cut into bite sized cubes
1 tbsp dried shrimp
a handful of bean sprouts
1 tbsp roasted peanuts, crushed
1 lime wedge
1 tsp chilli powder

Soak the noodles in water for 2 hours until soft. Drain the noodles and set aside. Simmer the fish sauce, tamarind water, and palm sugar for 2 minutes until the sugar is dissolved.

Heat oil in a wok over medium heat and fry shallots and cooked prawns until fragrant. Add the egg and stir-fry together with the tofu and dried shrimp. When cooked, add the noodles and turn up the heat to stir-fry for 2 minutes, allowing the noodles to take on a nice dark brown colour. Pour in the prepared sauce and add the bean sprouts and Chinese chives. Cook for 2 minutes then take off the heat and toss with the nuts and a pinch of chilli powder. Garnish with the nuts and the chilli powder before serving.

Mango sticky rice

This dish is the most popular dessert in Thailand. Fresh mango is best paired with sticky rice cooked in coconut milk. This softens and sweetens the sticky rice, giving it a rice pudding-like texture.

This dish is traditionally served during the Thai summer months of April and May (which is delicious honey mango season too!)

Serves 4

2 ripe honey mangoes or ripe mangoes
1 cup of sticky rice
1 cup of coconut milk
3 tbsp coconut cream
3 tbsp sugar
½ tsp salt
a few orchid flower or edible flower for garnish
To make the blue plate, see page 36

Soak the sticky rice in cold water for at least 3-4 hours or overnight. Drain and rinse thoroughly. Line a steamer with a muslin cloth and place the rice on top. Bring the water in the steamer to the boil and steam the rice over a medium heat for 15 -20 minutes. Then stand for 10 minutes to rest. Set aside.

Combine the coconut milk and sugar in a small pan and heat gently, stirring all the time, until the sugar has dissolved. Do not boil. Stir the salt and pour over the cooked rice, stirring gently, set aside to cool.

Peel the mangoes and cut off the skin and slice each piece of fruit into thin lengthways slices.

Put a mound of rice on a dish lined with the slices of mango and pour the coconut cream over the rice. Garnish with flowers and serve immediately.

Vietnam

A Warrior's bapssang

One of Vietnam's most well-known figures is Ho Chi Minh, who led the country in a fight for independence during the Vietnam War. But one figure whom many foreigners may not recognize is Vo Nguyen Giap. He was a general in the Vietnam People's Army and this is an incredible story of a hero who saved the nation from a crisis of desperation.

Giap had a legendary military career that saw him fight against the French before and after the Second World War; the Japanese during the Second World War; America, in the infamous Vietnam War; and Cambodia and China, in the Cambodian-Vietnamese War. He was proudly patriotic with a background in journalism, law, and history. This experience helped foster the strong leadership skills and tactical mind that allowed him to defeat some of the most militarily advanced countries of the day.

I was so fascinated to learn how a humble, ordinary citizen became a military genius and saved his country. I wondered where his sense of courage, perseverance, and self-sacrifice came from. He was rebellious from a young age, and though he had no formal military training, his experience in a guerrilla group allowed him to rise through the military ranks to be considered one of the world's best strategists.

Giap was a charismatic, courteous, clean-living man who inspired resourcefulness and loyalty in a small and seemingly powerless country. He is still considered a national hero of the Vietnamese people: a man who led the country to victory and independence alongside Ho Chi Minh.

Vietnamese food

Chaotic, messy, and colourful, the traditional Vietnamese street market is one of my favourite places to be. It's a colourful array of fresh vegetables, fruit, herbs, fresh fish and meat, all laid out in rows of small vendors serving delicious hot food. It's simple cooking that uses extremely fresh ingredients to result in incredible and often unusual flavours.

Walking around Hanoi in the early evening, you will find all types of delicious street food. The city is a melting pot of European and Indochinese flavours. Here you can find charcoal-braised sizzling Satay, Banh mi (a Vietnamese delicacy featuring a French baguette with roast meat and savoury pickle); caramelised pork Bun Cha; or the nation's favourite, Pho, each served on every corner of the block.

These authentic local and regional food vendors are able to coexist with modern high-rise buildings and world food giants like Starbucks, McDonald's and KFC. I think that the Vietnamese Street food offered is humble, incredible, delicious and is remarkable for maintaining a low price. It makes Western fast food pale in comparison.

I am stunned by the street food, the local market, and small restaurants with such a variety of simple but utterly honest food. Whenever I'm there, I stop by to try their specialties and, if I am lucky, I will get their secret recipes, passed down through the generations.

A Warrior's bapssang:

Pho
Banh mi
Cha ca la vong
Sticky rice in lotus leaf
Prawn rice paper rolls
Eel salad
Vietnamese papaya salad
Infused silken tofu with pandan leaves

Pho

Pho is Vietnamese soul food that is eaten all round the clock: whether early in the morning, at lunchtime, or dinnertime. This bowl of noodle soup is very popular across Asia and consists of a warm clear soup with rice noodles, thin sliced meat and vegetables, topped with a bunch of herbs and a drop of spicy and sour dip. It's the perfect thing on a rainy day to warm up the body.

Serves 4-6

FOR THE BROTH:

3 kg beef bones (marrow and knuckle bones)
12 litres water
5 star anises
10 cardamom pods
3 cinnamon sticks
10 black peppercorns
1 whole garlic, cut lengthwise
2 medium-sized onions
1 small ginger
1 tbsp salt
4 tbsp fish sauce
a small rock sugar
100g rice noodle
1 kg sirloin
1 onion, thinly sliced
100g beansprout
1 fresh green chilli, thinly sliced
1 fresh red chilli, thinly sliced
1 lime, sliced
salt and pepper

FOR THE GARNISH:

a bunch of herbs (like mint, coriander, holy basil, dill and spring onion)

FOR THE DIP:

3 tbsp fish sauce
1 tbsp sugar
1 fresh lime, squeezed
1 chilli, chopped

To prepare the Pho broth, char the onion and ginger on a gas stove. Place onions and ginger on the cooking grate and let skin burn. After around 15 minutes, they will soften and become sweetly fragrant. Use tongs to occasionally rotate them. You do not have to blacken the entire surface, just enough to slightly cook the onion and ginger.

Heat the star anise, cardamom, cinnamon, and whole black pepper on a hot frying pan for a few minutes, just enough to release their fragrances. Allow to cool.

Under warm water, remove the charred onion skin; trim and discard blackened parts of the root and stem ends. If ginger skin is puckered and blistered, smash ginger with the flat side of a knife to loosen flesh from the skin. Otherwise, use a sharp paring knife to remove the skin, running the ginger under warm water to wash off the blackened bits. Set aside.

Place bones in a stockpot and cover with cold water. Bring to a boil over a high heat. Boil for 2–3 minutes to allow the impurities to be released. Dump bones and water into the sink and rinse the bones with warm water. Quickly scrub the stockpot to remove any residue and return the bones to the pot.

Add water to the pot along with the bones, the sirloin, charred onion, ginger, and roasted spices and bring to boil, then lower the flame to gently simmer. Use a ladle to skim any dark foam that rises to the surface. Add remaining broth ingredients and cook uncovered for an hour and a half on low heat. Remove the sirloin (the meat should be medium rare) and place in a bowl of cold water for 10 minutes to chill and stop it cooking. Then refrigerate the meat to keep it chilled. Allow broth to continue cooking. In total, the broth should simmer for 3 hours.

Strain the broth through a fine strainer and use a ladle to skim as much fat from the top of the pho broth as you like. Taste and adjust the flavour with the additional salt, fish sauce and rock sugar if necessary.

To make the dip, add the dip ingredients to a mixing bowl and whisk well until the sugar is dissolved.

Retrieve the chilled sirloin and cut it into thin slices.

Cook the noodles for 3-5 minutes and then add the bean sprouts for around 1 minute to blanch. Pour into a bowl and place slices of meat and a ladleful of broth over the noodles. Garnish with the onion, chillies, herbs and serve with dips.

Banh mi

The French left their culinary impression on Vietnam with this tasty dish: a baguette with an Asian-style meat. The meat is marinaded and charcoal cooked with spicy, sweet and sour pickles and herbs. I lost count of the number of times I had banh mi while I was in Vietnam. There was such joy in walking around, eating it with a big open mouth without feeling shame of eating on the street. It was so great. This wonderful dish of pâté, and grilled meat (chicken, pork, or beef) can be found in many varieties on any street in Vietnam. It's just so tasty.

Serves 4

300g rump steak
2 shallots, chopped
1 tsp garlic, minced
3 lemongrass stems, white part only, roughly chopped
1 red chilli, chopped
2 tbsp fish sauce
a pinch of toasted sesame seeds
a handful of coriander sprigs
1 red chilli, chopped for a garnish
2 large French baguettes with ends cut off, cut again into 4 lengths

FOR THE PICKLE:
½ mooli, peeled and julienne
½ cucumber, peeled and julienne
1 carrot, peeled and julienne
¼ cup of rice vinegar
¼ cup of sugar
¼ tsp salt

Thinly slice the steak and place in a bowl. Place the shallots, garlic, lemongrass, and chilli in a mortar or food processor to grind the mixture into a fine paste. Add the fish sauce and sesame seeds to the mixture. Toss the mixture over the meat. Cover and refrigerate for an hour. Cook the meat in a hot frying pan for 2–3 minutes or until the meat is cooked.

Combine the sugar, rice vinegar, and salt in a small bowl and whisk until the sugar has completely dissolved. Then add the mooli, the cucumber, and the carrot.

Lay out the baguettes and split them lengthways. Place the meat and pickles within and garnish with chilli and coriander before serving.

Cha ca la vong

This very unique dish is a Vietnamese-style hot pot, with fish coated in turmeric and lots of herbs served with noodles and a pungent roasted peanut dip. Throughout Asia, hot pots are very popular, cooked with thinly sliced meat, seafood, and arrays of vegetables. It's unusual to find a hot-pot like this, with fish or other seafood, nevertheless, Cha ca la vong is one of the most iconic dishes of Hanoi and a great way to enjoy fish hot-pot style!

Serves 4-6

500g firm white fish fillet (ling, cod, or monkfish for example) skinned and cut into 10cm pieces

1 tsp turmeric powder

2 tbsp flour (for dusting)

3 tbsp oil

salt and pepper

FOR THE DIPPING SAUCE:

1 tbsp shrimp paste

4 tbsp lime juice

4 tbsp water

1 tbsp fish sauce

2 tsp sugar

2 tsp garlic, minced

1 thai chilli

salt and pepper

FOR THE NOODLES:

10–15 stalks of spring onion cut into 10cm pieces

a handful of dill cut into 10cm pieces

175g vermicelli noodles

a handful of roasted peanuts, roughly chopped

a handful of roughly torn mixed herbs (mint, coriander and Thai basil)

3 Thai chillies, chopped

a few lemon wedges

Mix the fish with turmeric in a bowl and season with the salt and pepper. Cover and refrigerate for 1 hour.

To make the dipping sauce, use a pestle and mortar to crush the garlic and chilli together into a paste. Add the fish sauce and the sugar and mix well to dissolve the sugar. Then add the water, lime juice, and shrimp paste. It should taste sweet and sour, and very savoury.

Bring a pan of water to a boil and drop the noodles in. Take off the heat and rinse in cold water before draining, then transfer to a serving bowl. Add the peanuts in a small serving dish with the fresh mixed herbs. Mix the dipping sauce ingredients and lay aside in a third bowl.

Sift the flour before dusting the fish, tossing the pieces just enough so that they are well covered. Heat the oil in a medium-sized frying pan and cook the fish until it has turned golden and crispy. Add the dill and spring onion to the pan and cook for 1 minute or until wilted.

Add the cooked fish, wilted spring onion, and dill to the serving bowl (use a large bowl if you have one). Serve with the noodles, the peanuts, and the dipping sauce in separate bowls for people to help themselves from. If desired, you can cook this using a portable gas stove at the table to serve it warm and share with others.

Sticky rice in lotus leaf

In the Middle East, the traditional stuffed dish uses peppers, tomatoes or even vine leaves. In Asia, it is typically lotus leaves that are stuffed, commonly with meats, like pork or chicken. But I would like to introduce you to this vegetarian style dish that is inspired by one that I once had in a temple.

Serve 4

100g glutinous rice
100g short grain rice
1 tbsp black sticky rice
1 potato, diced
½ tsp salt
5 dry shiitake mushrooms
1 tbsp Borlotti beans, cooked
1 shallot, diced
1 tbsp soy sauce
2 large, dried lotus leaves, cut into 3 pieces each

FOR THE GARNISH:

1 tbsp edamame beans, cooked
4 tbsp toasted peanut powder

Soak the rice in cold water for around 2 hours. Drain the rice and rinse it under cold running water until the water runs clear. Set aside.

Soak the dried mushrooms in warm water for 20 minutes. Drain and squeeze out any excess water before slicing them.

Heat the oil in a frying pan and cook the shallots until soft. Add the mushrooms and sauté for around 3–5 minutes, then season with the soy sauce, salt, and pepper. Remove from the heat and allow it to rest.

Soak the dried lotus leaves in warm water until soft.

Place the rice in a bowl with the mushroom mixture, potato, and beans and toss together. Divide the rice into 6 portions.

Lay the leaf vein side down on a surface and place the rice in the centre of the leaf, fold and lightly press down to make a parcel. Wrap in a string and then steam for 20 minutes.

Remove from the heat and carefully cut to serve. Garnish with the edamame beans and peanut powder and serve.

Prawn rice paper rolls

This rice roll features prawns and noodles wrapped with the bright and fresh flavours of colourful vegetables and herbs and served with a creamy and nutty dip. It's just perfect as an appetizer. It's an incredibly versatile dish that you can make with meat, fish, or vegetables; you could even make a vegan version, or one that's gluten free. You can create it your way.

Serves 4-6

24 cooked prawns, peeled and cut in half lengthways

100g vermicelli rice noodles

24 rice papers

2 small iceberg lettuces, torn

1 ripe pineapple, cut into 5cm batons

a handful of herbs (coriander, mint, and holy basil)

half an apple, cored and sliced

half an avocado, cored and sliced

a few chillies, chopped

FOR THE DIP:

⅓ cup creamy peanut butter

2 tbsp rice vinegar

1 tbsp sesame oil

2 tbsp water

1 tbsp minced garlic

2 tbsp sugar

1 tbsp vegetable oil

1 tsp lime juice

1 tbsp roughly chopped roasted peanut

Soak the rice vermicelli in boiling water for around 3–5 minutes, gently stirring to separate the noodles. Drain and refresh under cold water.

Dip a rice paper in warm water for 1 second, do not soak it longer or it will ruin easily being too soft and liable to tear when rolled.

Place the paper on a flat surface. Then place the lettuce, noodles, pineapple, apple, avocado, chilli, herbs, and prawns in the middle of the paper and fold in the left and right sides. Lift the bottom edge up and over the filling. Tightly roll over to enclose the filling completely. Continue rolling as tightly as possible. Cover with a damp towel and refrigerate until ready to serve.

In a food processor, combine the peanuts, garlic, oil, sugar, lime juice and sesame oil, and process until the mixture forms a fine paste. It should be smooth and creamy. Transfer to a small sauce bowl garnished with the peanuts.

Cut each roll into bite sized pieces and serve with the dip.

Eel salad

Eel. When I first mentioned this dish to my customers some of them were a little scared, but, since then, they have tasted the dish and changed their minds. I think it's because it is such a delicious, smoky, tender meat that goes perfectly with a caramelised sauce.

Serves 4

2 packs of cooked eels, cut into bite sized chunks

1 shallot, finely chopped

2 lemongrass stems, white part only, freshly chopped

1 red chilli, seeded and finely chopped

3 garlic cloves, finely chopped

1 tbsp fish sauce

1 tbsp sesame oil

4 tbsp roasted peanuts, roughly chopped

1 handful of coriander and mint, roughly torn

4 rice papers

salt and pepper

Heat oil in a deep-frying pan or wok, deep-fry the rice paper for a few seconds and drain on a paper towel. Leave to cool.

Heat a little oil in a wok and stir-fry the garlic, shallots, lemongrass, and chilli for around 2–3 minutes until it becomes fragrant. Add the eel and toss gently for a few seconds. Switch off the heat, then season with the fish sauce, soy sauce, sesame oil, salt, and pepper. To serve, toss with the peanuts, coriander, and mint before garnishing with the deep-fried rice paper to serve.

Vietnamese papaya salad

This is another version of the papaya salad, which uses mango and other fruit. It's bursting with ripe exotic fruit and lightly cooked prawns and is served with vegetables, herbs, and crunchy nuts. A sweet and sour, delightfully light salad.

Serves 4

24 cooked prawns, peeled and cut in half lengthways

1 shallot, peeled and julienne

1 carrot, peeled and julienne

1 firm mango, peeled and julienne

½ cucumber, seeded and julienne

1 red pepper, seeded and julienne

1 cup pomelo flesh

1 chilli, seeded and julienne

½ cup roasted peanut, roughly broken

a bunch of herbs, roughly torn

FOR THE DRESSING:

3 tbsp fish sauce

a freshly squeezed lime

1 tsp rice vinegar

3 tbsp sugar

2 garlic cloves, finely chopped

1 red chilli, finely chopped

Combine the fish sauce, lime juice, rice vinegar, and sugar in a small bowl and stir until the sugar has completely dissolved. Put the prawns, shallot, carrot, mango, cucumber, pepper, pomelo and chilli in a bowl. Pour in the dressing and gently toss with the nuts and herbs, then serve.

Infused silken tofu with pandan leaves

You sweat a lot when you're walking around in hot weather, and you definitely need a cold drink to cool down. This sweetened tofu is a wonderfully tasty way to cool down. The silken tofu is infused with fragrant pandan leaves and a kick of ginger making it so refreshing in the boiling hot summer of Vietnam.

Serves 4-6

500g silken tofu
300g sugar
500ml water
a small fresh ginger
1 mandarin juiced
1 tbsp green tea leaves
5 pandan leaves (4 for garnish)

Put the sugar and 500ml of water in a saucepan and slowly bring to the boil, stirring until the sugar has dissolved. Add the mandarin juice, ginger and 1 of the pandan leaves and simmer for 5 minutes to make a syrup. Strain and then return to the saucepan.

Roughly break the silken tofu and add to the saucepan with the syrup and leave it for at least 15 minutes to allow the tofu to absorb the flavours. Then chill before serving in a small bowl garnished with the remaining pandan leaves.

Malaysia

Let's go to Penang

Penang has fabulous street food and grand heritage sites. It's full of beautiful projects for recycling and reinvention. I was so inspired by the way the old slums have been turned into one of the world's most famous places for graffiti. It's marvellous to see waste turned into valuable artworks.

Only a few minutes away from Penang, you find local exotic flowers everywhere. The scent of hibiscus flowers surrounded me and mango trees, covered in fresh mangoes stood all around. On the same lane were papaya, banana, and coconut trees.

I didn't know what to say. It was such beautiful scenery for a chef. I have always dreamt of finding luxurious exotic ingredients so easily. Fancy a papaya salad for lunch? Easy, let's just pick some straight from the garden. Mango lassi? Let's pick some of that too!

The true beauty of Malaysia is found in the sheer diversity of its religion, cultures, and architecture. The street food of Malaysia reflects the shared heritages of these people and their beliefs and culture, which distinguishes Malaysian cuisine. In George Town, for instance, you can find Muslim mosques, Buddhist and Hindu temples, and Christian churches all coexisting on one street, the 'Street of Harmony'. Many Malay, Indians, and Chinese live here peacefully.

George Town was founded by the British East India Company in 1786 and named after King George III. It's now a UNESCO world heritage site where the local council works alongside citizens, young artists, architects and designers to create a beautiful city. In 2012, Ernest Zacharevic was commissioned by the Penang municipal council to create a street art project called 'Mirrors George Town' which consisted of painting several large-scale murals in different locations of the old town. This extraordinary project is now a famous landmark and has made locals proud and the town a must-see for tourists.

Malay food

Malaysian food uniquely blends national identities. The base of South East Asian seasoning is fish sauce, palm sugar, shrimp paste, spices, and soy sauce. The cultural diversity from citizens of Indian, Chinese and Malay descent heavily influence the local food.

Chinese noodle soup infused with local Malay ingredients, and Indian spices give rise to dishes like Penang Laksa, or Curry Mee. Bedding of coconut rice with spiced chicken, crunchy anchovies, nuts, and fiery hot sambal sauce is the identity of the Malaysian national dish called 'Nasi Lemak'.

Penang's heritage food

Celebrating 3 cultures

Asam laksa
Curry mee
Satay
Nasi lemak
Black pepper crab
Salad with noodles
Clay pot rice with chicken, Chinese sausage and greens
Exotic fruits with ice cream and sorbet

Asam laksa

Laksa typically consists of rice noodles in a thick soup, made from either coconut milk, curry paste, or tamarind, in a fish based soup, depending on the local ingredients.

Laksa's origins lie in the 15th century from the Ming dynasty, when Chinese traders came to the Malaysian cities of Malacca and Penang - both major stops on the spice route to Europe. Laksa is culturally embraced in multiple regions throughout South Asia.

Penang's Asam laksa has sweet and sour, spicy and umami flavours all in one soup. The key to success with traditional laksa is the very particular umami flavour that comes from the ginger torch flower. The ginger torch flower is difficult to find, but don't worry, I created another way to release the fragrant umami taste.

Serves 4

4 mackerel fillets with their skin on (reserve bones, head for stock)

6 cups of water

12 fish balls (available from Asian mart)

1 small ginger, sliced

4–5 pieces Asam Keping (dried tamarind slices)

5 tbsp tamarind juice

400g thick rice noodles (laksa noodles)

salt and sugar to taste

1 shallot, cut into half

2 lemongrass stalks, bruised

2.5cm size fresh galangal

4 dried chillies

1 fresh red chilli, chopped

1 tsp dried shrimp paste

1 tbsp flour for dusting

FOR THE GARNISH:

½ fresh pineapple, peeled and julienne

½ cucumber, seeded and julienne

½ onion, peeled and thinly sliced

1 red chilli, sliced

a few sprigs of mint leaves, torn

1 lime, sliced

4 dried red chillies

First, using kitchen tongs, cook the shallots and ginger on a stove flame until burnt. In a pot of water add the lemongrass, galangal, shrimp paste, fish bones, and heads, dried chillies, and fresh chillies, with the burnt shallots and ginger and bring to the boil for 30 minutes. Then strain the stock to another large pot and add tamarind juice and sugar to taste. Add the Asam Keping and simmer for 20-30 minutes in medium heat until the soup thickens slightly and add salt for taste.

Blanch the flat rice noodles in boiling water, drain in cold water and set aside.

Heat oil in a frying pan. Meanwhile, pat the mackerel fillet dry and lightly dust with the flour. Place the mackerel skin-side down in the hot oil and cook for 3–4 minutes until the fish is golden brown, then turn over and continue cooking for another 3–4 minutes. Remove from the heat and set aside.

Place noodles in a bowl and ladle the soup over it. Put the fish and a pinch of each garnishing ingredient over the top.

Curry mee

This is a real harmony dish, celebrating Penang street food influenced by Malay, Chinese and Indian residents alike. Complete with its South Indian curry paste, Chinese long-loving noodles and local Malay ingredients, this dish quickly became one of Penang's most popular dishes. Malaysians simply cannot resist this sour and spicy dish.

Serves 4

12 prawns
1 onion, sliced and cut
3 garlic cloves, peeled, finely chopped
1 tbsp ginger
1 lemongrass stalk, white part only, finely chopped
1 tbsp red curry paste
3 tbsp curry powder
½ tsp turmeric
1 can of coconut milk
3 tbsp fish sauce
1 tsp sugar
1 pack of thick rice noodles
a handful of bean sprouts
a handful of coriander leaves, torn
1 lime, sliced
1 red chilli, chopped

Heat the oil in a pot over a medium heat and add the onion, garlic, ginger, and lemongrass. Simmer for around 5 minutes until soft and fragrant. Add red curry paste and stir.

Turn the heat up to high and add the prawns, stir frying until they turn opaque. Add the curry powder, turmeric, coconut milk, fish sauce, and sugar then simmer for 10 minutes. Bring a pot of water to the boil to blanch the bean sprouts for a few seconds. Remove and drain with cold water, set aside.

Cook noodles in salted water for a few minutes, then plunge into cold water and drain.

Taste the stock and season with the salt and pepper. Divide the noodles into bowls and pour over the stock. Garnish with the prawns, bean sprouts, coriander, lime, and chilli before serving.

Satay

All throughout South East Asia, people argue about which satay dish is best or 'original'. To a foreigner's taste, all are delicious. The dish comprises meat marinated in fresh local ingredients and is cooked on a charcoal fire. It's so easy that you can find it everywhere, whether in a restaurant or on a street corner. It's just great food.

Peanut satay dressing

100g peanuts, finely ground
1 cup of coconut cream
½ cup of coconut milk
3 tbsp palm sugar
1 tbsp fish sauce
1 pandan leaf (optional)
1 dried red chilli soaked in warm water, chopped
1 tbsp coriander seeds
1 tbsp cumin seeds
1 tbsp lemongrass, chopped
1 tsp galangal, chopped
1 tbsp shallots, chopped
2 tbsp garlic, minced
1 tbsp water

Place the dried chilli, coriander and cumin seeds, galangal, shallots, garlic, and 1 tbsp water into a food processor and blitz until it has become a smooth paste.

Heat oil in a pan and fry the paste for around 4–5 minutes until fragrant and oily. Add the coconut cream and milk and cook for 10 minutes then stir in the palm sugar, the peanuts and pandan leaf. Season with the fish sauce and soy sauce. Simmer for 20 minutes on a medium heat until the liquid is of a thick consistency. Transfer to a serving bowl, serve with satay.

Beef satay

200g beef rump steak, trimmed and cut into cubes
3 tbsp soy sauce
1 freshly squeezed lime
1 tbsp brown sugar
1 tbsp minced garlic
1 tsp ginger
1 tbsp minced spring onion
24 bamboo skewers, soaked in water for 20 minutes

Whisk the soy sauce, lime juice, sugar, garlic, and ginger together in a bowl then add the beef, toss to coat completely, allow to marinate for 1 hour, thread the beef onto the skewers for 1 hour or overnight.

Pork satay

200g lean pork steak, cut into bitesize chunks
2 tbsp soy sauce
1 tbsp sesame oil
2 tbsp coconut cream
1 tbsp red curry paste
1 tbsp fish sauce
1 tbsp palm sugar
1 tbsp tamarind paste
3 tbsp chopped peanuts
24 bamboo skewers, soaked in water for 20 minutes

Mix the meat with the soy sauce and sesame oil.

In a saucepan, combine the coconut cream and red curry paste, then cook for 5 minutes on a low heat. Add the fish sauce, palm sugar, tamarind paste and chopped peanuts. Cook for a further 5 minutes, then add the coconut milk, cool down, then add the pork mix. Let them marinate. Thread marinated meat and place in the fridge for at least 1 hour, or overnight.

Chicken satay

2 tbsp smooth peanut butter
2 tbsp soy sauce
1 freshly squeezed lime juice
1 tbsp soft dark brown sugar
2 tbsp curry powder
2 cloves of garlic, chopped
3 skinless, boneless chicken thighs, diced
3 skinless, boneless chicken breast fillets, diced
about 24 bamboo skewers, soaked in water for 20 minutes

In a mixing bowl, combine the peanut butter, soy sauce, lime juice, sugar, curry powder and garlic. Place the chicken in the marinade and onto bamboo skewers and refrigerate for at least 1 hours, overnight is best.

To finish the dishes

Preheat a grill or grill pan over a medium-high heat. Oil the grill racks and place the chicken, pork, and beef on the grill. Reserve the remaining juice from the meat for drizzling when serving. Cook the skewers for 2-3 minutes per side or until the meat is cooked. Remove from the heat. Lay the skewers onto a banana leaf (if desired) or on a serving platter and sprinkle with the remaining marinade over the skewers. Garnish with the peanut dressing. Serve immediately.

Nasi lemak

This is Malaysia's national favourite meal. Coconut rice and braised chicken in a mild curry cooked with fragrant pandan leaf. This unlikely dish is given a crunchy element by anchovies and peanut, and a bit of spice from the sambal sauce, then softened up with fresh cucumber and boiled egg.

It's a combination of everything to become one - Chinese, Malay, Indian – that makes 'Nasi Lemak' such a special dish.

Serves 4

8 chicken drumsticks
2 cups of plain yogurt
2 eggs
2 tbsp curry powder
1 tbsp turmeric powder
2 tsp salt
½ tsp sugar
vegetable oil for deep frying

FOR THE FLOUR MIXTURE:

1 cup of all-purpose flour
½ cup of rice flour
½ cup of corn starch
2 tsp curry spice mix
1 tsp black pepper
1 tsp baking powder

FOR THE RICE:

½ tsp salt
200ml can of coconut milk
a small piece of fresh ginger.
200g basmati rice
1 pandan leaf, tied in a knot

FOR THE SAMBAL SAUCE:

2 tbsp vegetable oil
1 onion, peeled, thinly sliced
1 garlic clove, finely chopped
1 tsp shrimp paste
1–2 tsp red chilli paste
100g dried anchovies, soaked in water and drained
1 tbsp sugar
3 tbsp tamarind puree

FOR THE GARNISH:

2 eggs
a handful of small, dried anchovies
a handful of toasted peanuts
½ cucumber, thinly sliced

Put the coconut milk, ginger, lemongrass, rice, and a pinch of salt in a large saucepan. Add 200ml water, stir and cook over medium heat for 10–15 minutes, or until the rice is cooked and all the liquid has been absorbed.

To make the sambal, heat the oil in a frying pan and sweat the onion and garlic for 5–7 minutes, until soft. Add the shrimp paste, chilli paste and most of the soaked anchovies and stir. Add the sugar and a pinch of salt and pour in the tamarind with 3 tbsp of water. Simmer until it reduces to a thick paste. Set aside.

In a small bowl, whisk together the ingredients for the curry mix. Set aside. Combine the chicken with the marinade in a bowl and leave to rest for 30 minutes in the fridge.

Mix the flour, egg, and a bit of cold water in a bowl to form a wet consistency. Add the drumstick into the mixture, gently shaking off the excess flour. In a deep frying pan, heat the oil to 170°C and deep fried the chicken until golden brown. Place the cooked chicken on a wire rack set over a kitchen towel.

To prepare the garnish, boil the eggs in water for 7–10 minutes - the yolks should be firm. When they are cool enough to handle, peel off the shells and cut the eggs in half. Heat the oil in a deep-fat fryer to 180°C and deep-fry the dried white anchovies for 3 minutes, or until crispy. Toast the peanuts in a dry frying pan.

Pick the lemongrass out of the rice and discard. Put the rice in a small bowl and press down until it is compacted. Upturn the rice in the middle of the pandan leaf. Arrange the egg, peanuts, cucumber and remaining anchovies around the rice and scatter over the crispy anchovies and serve.

Black pepper crab

This is one of the most memorable dishes that I had while I was in Chinatown, Kuala Lumpur. The crabs that I had from a humble street stall were fleshy and succulent, overwhelming with natural sweet tastes. It was such a pleasure.

Serves 4

4 Cornish crabs or blue swimming crabs
1 cup of vegetable oil
35g black peppercorns, lightly crushed
4 garlic cloves, sliced
5cm piece of ginger, peeled and sliced
½ bunch spring onions, sliced
2 long red chillies, thinly sliced
4 tbsp soy sauce
4 tbsp oyster sauce
2 tsp sugar
80g unsalted butter, chopped
½ cup chicken stock (optional) or water
a handful of coriander leaves
a pinch of sesame seed

To prepare the crabs, break off the tail flaps on the underside and discard. Carefully pull off the back shells and reserve. Remove gills from the meat and discard, then rinse and discard the stomach. Cut each crab in half lengthwise, then crack large claws to ensure they cook through. Pat the crabs dry using a paper towel.

Heat oil in a wok over high heat to 180°C. Add the crabs in batches and cook, turning occasionally, for 2 minutes or until just before cooked through. Using kitchen tongs, remove crabs and drain on a paper towel.

Remove half the oil from the wok and discard. Add the peppercorns, garlic, ginger, half the spring onions and half the chillies to the wok and cook, stirring for 1 minute or until fragrant. Add the soy sauce, oyster sauce, sugar, butter, and chicken stock and simmer for 1 minute. Return the crabs to the wok and simmer, turning occasionally, for a further 4 minutes or until the sauce has reduced. Top with remaining spring onions, chillies, and coriander leaves. Sprinkle with sesame seed and serve immediately.

Salad with noodles

Vibrant Malay noodle salad.

Bursting with incredible colours this dish is light and refreshing. Seasoned with a South Eastern style dressing, you'll find delicious prawns, vegetables, fresh fruit, a bunch of herbs, and crunchy nuts to finish. If you think you've had too much spicy food, this is a dish you should try.

Serves 4

300g fresh prawn cooked, peeled

100g thin rice noodles

3 tomatoes, seeded and thinly sliced

1 red pepper, seeded and thinly sliced

½ mango, seeded and thinly sliced

1 apple, cored and thinly sliced

1 red onion, peeled and thinly sliced

a handful of mixed fresh herbs (spring onion, coriander, mint, basil), torn

1 tbsp fried shallots

3 tbsp roasted peanuts, roughly chopped

3 kaffir lime leaves, julienne

FOR THE DRESSING:

3 tbsp fish sauce

2 tbsp lime juice

1 lemongrass stalk, white part only, minced

1 red chilli, chopped

1 garlic clove, minced

1 tbsp minced shallots

3 tbsp palm sugar

Place the noodles into a pan of boiling water and cook for 4-5 minutes, stirring constantly. Drain and rinse under cold water. Set aside.

To make the dressing, mix the fish sauce, lime juice and sugar. Add the garlic, lemongrass, shallots, and chillies to a bowl with the noodles and the prawns. Mix thoroughly and toss gently with the last ingredients (the mixed herbs, pepper, tomatoes, red onion, fruit, fried shallots, and peanuts). Serve.

Clay pot rice with chicken, Chinese sausage and greens

I first had this dish a long time ago when I was in Malaysia. I stopped by a guy surrounded by wonderful fragrances who had set up a charcoal fire on the side of the street and was cooking with around 12–15 clay pots at the same time as controlling the fire. It was mad, multi-task cooking. Charcoal-cooked clay pot rice is at once fluffy and crispy and goes perfectly with caramelised chicken, Chinese sausage and vegetables.

Serves 4

4 chicken thighs, skinned and cut into cubes
2 tbsp soy sauce
1 tbsp sugar
1 tbsp honey
1 tbsp minced garlic
a pinch of pepper
4 pak choi, torn
2 Chinese sausages, sliced
4 tbsp spring onion, chopped
2 cups long-grain Jasmine rice, washed and drained
4 cups of chicken stock

Heat oil in a large clay pot (or any other pot if you don't have a clay pot) and toast the rice for around 5 minutes, tossing frequently until the rice starts to turn translucent. Add the stock and bring to a boil. Cover, and cook for 10 minutes on a high heat. Then reduce the heat and continue to cook for another 10 minutes.

In a small bowl, combine the chicken with soy sauce, sugar, garlic, honey, and pepper. Mix well and allow to marinate for 10 minutes. Heat oil in a large frying pan. Fry the chicken for around 5 minutes or until it has caramelised and taken on a dark, golden colour. Remove from the pan and place on a plate. Allow to rest.

Heat oil in another frying pan and fry the sausage for about 1 minute on each side. Remove from the pan and place on a plate. Allow to rest.

To serve, place all ingredients - the chicken, the sausages, and pak choi - into the rice pot so the flavours can be absorbed by the rice. Garnish with a sprinkling of spring onion.

Exotic fruits with ice cream and sorbet

How much fruit do you eat? I hope that you eat as much as you can? I find that exotic fruits, being exceptionally sweet, are so refreshing after a main course. They cleanse your palate. It's so fun to have lots of people sit around a table and cut pieces of fruit to serve with sorbet or ice cream.

Forget naughty chocolate, or cake, it's time for naturally sweet exotic fruits.

Serves 4-6

1 papaya, halved
1 pineapple, halved
1 mango, cut into chunks
1 dragon fruit
1 starfruit
1 persimmon
1 nectarine
1 plum
1 prickly pear
1 lemon
½ pomelo
a handful of raspberries
a handful of strawberries
a handful of cherries
1 scoop of coconut ice cream
1 scoop of strawberry or raspberry ice cream

FOR THE COCONUT ICE CREAM:

1 cup of milk
1 can of coconut cream
1 ½ cups of heavy cream
1 ½ cups of sweetened flaked coconut

FOR THE STRAWBERRY OR RASPBERRY SORBET:

1 cup of fresh or frozen strawberries, partially thawed
1 cup of fresh or frozen raspberries
1 cup of sugar
2 tsp vanilla extract

To make the coconut ice cream, combine the milk and coconut cream in a food processor or blender and mix thoroughly. Stir in cream and flaked coconut. Pour into the container of an ice cream maker and freeze according to the manufacturer's instructions.

Place raspberries in a blender; cover and pulse until chopped. Transfer to a large bowl, stir in sugar until dissolved. Stir in remaining sorbet ingredients until well mixed. Pour mixture into an ice cream maker and freeze according to the manufacturer's directions. Transfer ice cream to freezer containers, allowing room for expansion. Freeze for around 2–4 hours or until firm.

To prepare the fruit, lay whole strawberries, raspberries and cherries on a large plate or bowl. The nectarine, plum, and star fruit should be cut into bitesize chunks. The dragon fruit, persimmon, prickly pear should be peeled and cut. The papaya and mango should be peeled with seeds removed, then cut into chunks. The pineapples needs a bit more work, cutting the skin and removing the hard inside. Once the fruit is exposed, cut into small pieces. For the pomelo: peel off the hard skin then break apart the segments. You can squeeze fresh lemon over the fruit for added sharpness.

China

Upside-down double fortune

Fortune. Everyone loves fortune, but the Chinese love it more than others, because for them, fortune is not just about money, it's about being fortunate: lucky. Why is that?

The story of the upside-down double fortune symbol began back in the Ming dynasty (14th -17th century) during the reign of its founder Empress Ma, the most beloved Empress of China.

Empress Ma and her husband, the Hongwu Emperor, both came from a humble background. The emperor was an extraordinary man who, with the help of his wife, rose from obscurity as a simple beggar to become the leader of China

Empress Ma

Once her husband became emperor, he grew increasingly vicious, using his power to kill many people. Empress Ma was the only one brave enough to stand up to him. One day the emperor went out for his inspection tour. When he arrived at a town, he saw a crowd of people laughing at a painting. The painting was of a woman from the west province refusing to have her feet bound and featuring a bare-footed woman holding a large watermelon in her arms.

The emperor thought the woman was his wife, who had not had her feet bound, and therefore that the people were mocking her. He was angered, and in response he sent his soldiers to write the character 'Fu' on the doors of those who did not join the crowd.

The people who did not have the character on their door were to be killed the next day.

When the Empress Ma learned about this, she quickly ordered everyone in the city to put a 'Fu' on their doors overnight.

As a result, all households followed her instructions. However, one of the families, who could not recognize the characters, accidentally painted it upside down. On the next day, the leader of the army reported to the emperor that the entire city had been marked with 'Fu', saying one of the families had the character upside down.

The emperor was very angry and instructed the army to kill the whole family. Empress Ma immediately said to the emperor, 'the family members know of your visit today and deliberately put the word 'Fu' upside down, which means fortune is arriving'.

The emperor was happy with her explanation and decided not to kill the family or the people who had mocked his wife. Since then, this has become a common Chinese New Year practice. The characters are written on red paper, considered to be a lucky colour, with two 'Fu' for a double fortune.

Chinese Tradition

Thinking about Chinese food, I was stuck. How on earth could I select only ten dishes?

I thought that it would be too difficult to choose the best dishes to celebrate - they're all so good!

As a result of there being too much choice, I decided to go for two themes that would enable me to introduce you to their culture and food. These themes are the Chinese New Year menu and the 1920s in Shanghai – a festival menu celebrating a new hope following the First World War. Just like Paris in the 1920s, the people living in Shanghai at this time greeted the decade with happiness and freedom of expression.

The Chinese New Year menu embodies the real Chinese spirit. It's a time of variety, family gatherings, and for respecting long-held Traditions. Giving lucky money in red envelopes to kids for good luck, and in return they kneel and bow and say 'Kung Hei Fat Choy'. This is a traditional way of wishing happiness and prosperity in the new lunar year. It's done by younger family members who bow in respect to their elders and to bid them an everlasting prosperity consisting of a blissful, abundant fortune.

Chinese food

The main seasoning in Chinese food is soy sauce, fermented bean pastes, and oyster sauce. Common techniques include smoking and cooking at high temperatures for a super crispy skin in meat dishes - like in Peking duck and chicken or pork dishes. One of the most popular dishes includes hot pot, where sliced meat, fish, vegetables, and tofu are cooked in a hot soup with dips. As popular as it is, that recipe will have to wait for another cookbook.

'Lucky Seven' New Year menu

Dumpling
Sticky rice balls
Wonton soup
Glutinous rice cake
Spring roll
Noodle
Steamed whole fish

Celebrations menu

Stir fried rice
Babao chai, 8 treasure dish
Peking duck
Mapo tofu
Burnt pork belly

Dumpling

Dumplings mean 'wealth' due to their traditional gold/silver ingot shape.

Every New Year, all family members sit down on the floor to make dumplings. It is the first thing to do on New Year's Eve, before celebrating the New Year. No matter how many get made they easily vanish: everyone loves the dumplings! Whether they are steamed, pan fried or deep fried, this is one we all love to eat. Make an occasion of it, gathering around your friends and family to make your own.

Serves 4-6

¼ Chinese cabbage, thinly sliced
a small handful of chives, finely chopped
100g minced pork
100g minced beef
2cm piece ginger, finely grated
1 garlic clove, minced
2 tbsp soy sauce
1 tbsp sesame oil
2 tsp sugar
salt and pepper
30-36 dumpling/wonton wrappers
1 tbsp vegetable oil, plus extra for frying

Combine the cabbage and chives together with the ginger, garlic, and sesame Oil. Combine with the minced pork and beef. Slap the mixture, picking it up and throwing it back into the bowl until it becomes smoother and firmer. Then season with the soy sauce, sugar, salt, and pepper. Cover with cling film and keep it in the fridge for at least 30 minutes.

Scoop a small teaspoonful of the filling into the centre of each dumpling skin. Damp the edges with water then fold the wrapper over the filling, firmly pressing the edges to seal.

Heat the vegetable oil in a heavy-bottomed saucepan over a high heat. Place the dumpling in the pan and fry for 2 minutes or until the bottom is crisp. Reduce the heat and add 2 tablespoons of water. Cover the pan and allow the dumpling to steam in the pan. Then serve.

Sticky rice balls

A sweet, nutty, runny filling in rice balls.

These balls of glutinous rice are filled with black sesame paste and tossed into simmering hot water and served with a simple syrup. Known for symbolizing harmony and togetherness, these are perfect for a family reunion.

Serves 4

1 cup of glutinous rice flour
½ cup warm water
50g roasted black sesame seeds
⅓ cup sugar
a small knob of butter

In a food processor or blender, grind the sesame seeds, the caster sugar. Use a spatula to mix them together in the food processor as you go. Then add the butter and pulse for 10 seconds at a time until the mixture is well combined. Scoop everything out into a bowl and put in the refrigerator for about 30 minutes.

Put the glutinous rice flour into a mixing bowl. Slowly add in the warm water while stirring to form a dough. The dough can't be too wet, or it will not hold its shape. Cover with a damp towel.

Add it to the boiling water and cook the piece of dough until it floats. Scoop it out and add it to the rest of the dough. Mix the two parts together until the dough is soft and smooth. Divide the dough into 12 equal pieces. Roll the filling into small marble-sized balls. Then take each dough ball and flatten into a circle about 2 inches in diameter. Add the filling to the centre, and close the dough over the filling. Roll the ball around in your hands until it's smooth and round. Repeat until all the sesame balls are made.

Bring a medium pot of water to a boil. Add the sesame balls and stir immediately to prevent them from sticking to each other. Serve the sesame balls in a bit of the hot water!

Wonton soup

Similar to dumplings, but the wonton is made of paper thin, square shaped wrappers instead of round. It is served in broth with some vegetables.

Serves 4

Wonton stock
2 cups of chicken stock
2 tbsp soy sauce
1 tsp salt
a pinch of ground white pepper
4 bunches of pak choi, leaves separated, or baby spinach

FOR THE WONTONS:
50g mince pork
5 dried shiitake mushrooms
12 raw prawns
½ tsp sesame oil
1 tbsp minced garlic
1 spring onion, chopped
12 wonton wrappers
a pinch of sugar
a pinch of salt, and white pepper
1 tsp minced ginger
½ tbsp soy sauce

To make the wontons, soak the dried mushrooms in warm water for 20 minutes. Drain, then squeeze out any excess water. Remove the stems and chop the caps.

Peel, devein, and roughly chop the prawns.

Place the prawns in a bowl with the mushrooms, garlic, ginger, spring onion, sesame oil, sugar, salt, and pepper and mix well. Mix in the pork and slap the mixture against the side of the bowl until it becomes firmer and stickier.

Lay out the wonton wrappers on a clean kitchen surface and spoon a teaspoon of the filling onto the centre of the wrapper. Dampen the edges of the wrapper, then fold it. Gather up the edges and twist to seal.

Meanwhile, bring stock to the boil and season with soy sauce, salt and pepper. Add the wontons to the water and after 3 minutes add the pak choi. Simmer for a few seconds, until wilted, then serve.

Glutinous rice cake

Chinese New Year sweet rice cakes are as much a staple as Christmas pudding is in the West.

They symbolise progress and growth. Sat around with the family, you can eat sweet rice cakes and talk about it in the hopes of having a better year ahead.

Serves 4-6

300g glutinous rice flour
110g wheat starch
a pinch of salt

FOR THE SUGAR MIX:
250g sugar
60g brown sugar
1½ cup of water
20g Chinese sesame paste

In a small saucepan, melt the sugar with cold water slowly over a medium heat. Remove from the heat, and let it cool.

Sift the rice flour and starch and gradually pour in the sugar. Add the salt and stir until smooth. If lumps persist, simply strain it with a sieve and then pour into the prepared cake pan lined with a little oil.

Prepare the steamer by bringing the water to a rolling boil. Give the batter a stir and pour into the prepared pan and cover with aluminium foil. Place inside the steamer and steam on high heat for 30 minutes and then lower the heat and steam for 1 hour. You may need to refill the water in the steamer throughout the cooking process. Don't let it dry out. Cool and serve.

Spring roll

Traditionally eaten during the 'Spring Festival', believed to bring wealth and prosperity in the New Year. Mixed with a variety of different vegetables, spring rolls are a popular starter or snack.

Serves 4-6

100g minced pork
1 tsp ginger juice
1 tbsp minced garlic
1 tbsp soy sauce
1 tsp sesame oil
a pinch of salt and pepper
2 spring onion, finely chopped
5g dried shiitake mushrooms, soaked in warm water for 20 minutes
100g Chinese cabbage, sliced
½ carrot, cut into julienne
100g bean sprout
8 spring roll wrappers
100g hoisin sauce

In a bowl add the minced pork, ginger, garlic, spring onion, salt, and pepper. Mix well and marinate for 30 minutes.

Drain the mushrooms and roughly chop.

Heat the oil in a frying pan, cook the pork for 3-5 minutes, then add the mushrooms and cook for another 5 minutes. Add the rest of other vegetables and cook until soft. Switch off the heat, add the soy sauce, sesame oil and check the seasoning. Add more the salt and pepper if it is required.

Lay a wrapper on a clean work surface and cover the remaining wrappers with a damp cloth. Have a bowl of cold water within reach. Put two teaspoons of filling in the middle and then fold the bottom point over the top of the filling. Roll it up to the middle of the sheet then fold the sides in over the top, wetting them slightly so they stick. Wet the top point, then roll up tightly. Repeat with the remaining wrappers and filling.

Heat a wok or large pan a third full of vegetable oil to 180°C, or until tiny bubbles gather around a dipped chopstick. Fry the spring rolls in batches of three or four, for about five minutes each, turning occasionally until golden and crisp. Drain on kitchen paper and serve with hoisin sauce.

Noodles

Long-life noodles are an essential dish to have on the New Year table. Soft noodles with with a selection of vegetables in warm broth. It's a hearty, soulful food for people across Asia.

Serves 4

4 cups of vegetable stock
200g so-mien noodles (thin noodles)
1 boneless chicken breast, shredded
1 pack of mixed wild mushrooms, torn
50g morning glory, chopped
1 tsp minced ginger
1 tbsp minced garlic
3 tbsp soy sauce
a small bunch of spring onion, roughly chopped (plus extra for the garnish)
a small bunch of morning glory, roughly chopped (plus extra for the garnish)
salt for seasoning

Pour the stock into a pan and add the chicken, mushrooms, ginger, and garlic. Bring to the boil, then reduce the heat. Partly cover and simmer for 20 minutes until the chicken is tender. Put the chicken on a board and shred into bite-size pieces using a fork.

Place the noodles into a pan of boiling water and cook for 4-5 minutes until it is cooked, stirring constantly. Drain, rinse under cold water and set aside.

Return the chicken to the stock, add the morning glory, mushrooms, spring onion, ginger and garlic and season with soy sauce and salt. Simmer for 3 minutes until the noodles are tender. Ladle into four bowls and scatter over the remaining spring onion and morning glory. Serve with extra soy sauce if you require.

Steamed whole fish

This is a delicious steamed fish recipe.

Made with a fresh whole fish steamed with plenty of green vegetables and shredded ginger, spring onion, coriander, touched with soy sauce, and vinegar. It's just so perfect. I highly recommend even staunch meat eaters to try this for the first time. While it seems like a lot of ingredients to find, you could use whatever you have in the fridge; you just need a good fresh fish.

Serves 2-4

1 whole sea bream descaled, scored head to tail, gutted

½ onion, sliced

a few leaves of white cabbage, sliced

5 spring onions, roughly chopped

3 Chinese leaves, sliced

1 potato, peeled, sliced

4 shiitake mushrooms, stemmed and thinly sliced

1 tsp toasted sesame oil

1 tbsp chopped fresh coriander, plus a few sprigs for garnish

1 lemon grass, trimmed and thinly sliced, or 2cm strips of lemon peel

2 spring onions, cut into thin strips about 4cm long

1 medium size red chilli, cut into thin slices

a small size of yellow pepper, cut into thin strips

ginger, thumb-sized, peeled and cut into thin strips

1 tbsp soy sauce

1 tsp rice wine vinegar

1 tbsp rice wine

4 slices of tofu (5 x 5cm)

1tbsp pickled olive leaves

salt and pepper

To make the vegetable stock, fill a large wok with 2 cups of water.

Add the Chinese cabbage, onion, cabbage leaves, spring onion, potato, and mushroom and to bring to the boil for 10 minutes.

Season the fish with the salt and pepper and coat both sides lightly with the sesame oil.

Place the fish into the wok and sprinkle in some lemongrass and scatter the spring onion and ginger on top of the fish. Drizzle with the soy sauce and vinegar and add the tofu. Turn down the heat to a steady simmer and cover the wok until the fish is cooked – about 10 to 15 minutes.

Transfer the fish into a large serving plate and scoop the stock over the fish and garnish with vegetables and herbs. Lay the tofu beside and garnish with pickle.

Stir fried rice

This simple dish is loved by everyone. I have never seen anyone who doesn't like it, meat eaters, pescatarians, vegetarians, vegans, and those on a gluten free diet. They absolutely love it. Fried rice is a good way to work in any leftovers, adding in lots of vegetables and flavouring it with soy sauce, oyster sauce, or a drizzle of sesame oil. You can even toss in chicken, shrimp, or whatever you like. The following recipe will get you started.

Serves 4-6

2 cups of cooked white rice
2 tbsp vegetable oil,
½ onion, finely chopped
½ carrot, peeled, chopped
2 spring onion, chopped
1 tsp soy sauce
1 tsp toasted sesame oil
salt and pepper
1 egg
4 tbsp frozen peas

Heat ½ tablespoon vegetable oil in a wok over a high heat until smoking and brown then add the onion and carrot and cook until it starts to soften. Add the cooked rice and stir and toss until the rice is a pale brown – about three minutes.

Press the rice up the sides of the wok so that you have space in the middle. Add the remaining ½ tablespoon oil to the space and break the egg into the oil and season with a little salt. Use a spatula to scramble the egg, breaking it up into small bits. Toss the egg and the rice together.

Add the frozen peas, spring onion, and continue to toss and stir until peas are thawed and every grain of rice is separate.

Serve immediately.

Babao chai, 8 treasure dish

Known as '8 treasure dish', this recipe celebrates the sea, fields, and mountain together. In it you'll find seafood, meat, greens and mountains vegetables create dish with prawns, squids, chicken and vegetables like mushrooms, pak choy, carrot, bamboo shoot seasoned with mainly oyster sauce.

Serves 4

2 shiitake mushrooms, sliced
2 bottom mushrooms, sliced
1 pak choi, sliced
¼ carrot, sliced
60g bamboo shoots,sliced
8 prawns, deshelled, cut into halves
80g squid skinned slices
1 chicken breast, sliced

FOR THE SAUCE:

2 tbsp veg oil
10g spring onion cut into 4cm length
a small piece of ginger, sliced
2 garlic cloves, sliced
1 tbsp rice wine
1 tbsp soy sauce
1 tbsp oyster sauce
1 tsp sesame oil
1 tbsp chilli oil
salt and pepper
starch water: ½ cup water add in 2 tbsp starch

In a large pan of boiling water, blanch the vegetables, remove, and plunge into ice water. Retain the boiling water and add the squid and prawns for 3-5 minutes until the prawn's colour turns opaque. Remove and place in the ice water. Next add the chicken, cooking for around 5 minutes before removing and plunging into the ice water. Drain and set aside.

In a large frying pan drizzle the veg oil and add the spring onion, ginger, and garlic and stir fry for 5 seconds. Then add the rice wine, soy sauce, oyster sauce, and chilli oil and add in the chicken, prawns, squid, and vegetables. Add the starch to the water. Season with salt and pepper and a drizzle of sesame oil, then serve.

Peking duck

Cooking the Peking duck at home is a real treat for your family and friends to share food on a day of occasion. It has an incredibly delicious smell that goes around the house making everyone hungry. Slow cooked and honey glazed, the Peking duck's skin is very crispy and the meat inside is tender. Served with a pancake, shredded cucumber, spring onion and a dense hoisin sauce, it is a true celebratory dish, one with a long history in China.

Serves 4-6

1 duck, fresh or frozen

FOR THE COATING:

1.5 litres of water

3 tbsp vinegar

3 tbsp maltose or honey

2 tbsp soy sauce

FOR THE MIXTURE:

3 tbsp Chinese five spice powder

2 tbsp salt

3 tbsp sugar

TO SERVE:

a bunch of spring onion, cut into julienne

1 cucumber, seeded, cut into julienne

20 Peking duck pancakes or thin bread

¼ cups hoisin sauce

Preheat the oven to 220°C/ Gas mark 7.

Bring the water and vinegar to the boil in a large pot. Hold the duck over the pot and, using a large ladle, carefully pour this mixture over the outside of the duck several times. Reserve the mixture. Hang the duck in a cool, airy place to dry overnight, or alternatively hang it in front of a cold fan for about 2-3 hours. When the duck is dried, bring the reserved water-vinegar liquid to the boil, add the maltose (or honey) and soy sauce and again, bathe the duck skin and leave to dry in front of the fan for at least 2-3 hours more. Once the duck has dried, the surface of the skin will dry. Mix the five-spice, sugar, and the salt together and rub this mixture evenly inside of the duck.

Place the duck on a roasting rack in a roasting pan, breast side up. Roast for 20 minutes, taking out at least twice to brush the vinegar mixture on the skin. This will help crisp the skin. Lower the oven temperature to 180°C and continue to roast for 1 hour.

Remove the duck from the oven and let it sit for at least 10 minutes before you carve it. Using a cleaver or a sharp knife, cut the skin and meat into pieces. Serve at once with the pancakes, spring onion, and cucumber with a bowl of hoisin sauce.

Mapo tofu

Sichuan is the western mountainous region of the Yangtze River. Sichuan cuisine developed in Sichuan province. The land is fertile and abundant with ingredients. The so-called 'heavenly bureau' is known for its spicy food.

The tofu which is most representative of Sichuan cuisine, is soft and spicy using two halves. In the Qing Dynasty, there was a woman named 'Onchyo' in Sacheon, who was widowed after 10 years of marriage. She ran a small restaurant where people called her 'Jean Mahapat' - her husband's surname was Jean, and he had a pitted face from smallpox.

The restaurant was mostly for the lower classes, and one day an old man came and ordered the tofu and ground meat. She felt sorry for the labourer who she could see worked hard, and so cooked with all sincerity. The resulting tofu dish became her most famous of dishes, and was eventually named 'Mapo tofu', meaning 'grandmother's tofu'. Today it an essential part of Sichuan cuisine and is a dish that supplements the energy of the body by preventing cold and sweating.

Serves 4-6

½ cup of chicken broth

2 tsp potato starch (half if using corn-starch)

2 tsp soy sauce

1 tsp sugar

1 tbsp sesame oil

2 medium cloves of garlic, minced

2 tsp minced ginger

4 green onions white part only, minced

1 tbsp fermented black beans, roughly chopped (black bean paste will also work)

½ tbsp Sichuan peppercorns, black seeds removed then ground (optional)

100g ground pork

2 tsp doubanjiang (chilli bean paste)

400g block of firm tofu, drained and cut into 1cm cubes

FOR THE GARNISH:

1 spring onion, chopped

½ red chilli, seeded, julienne

Add the chicken stock, corn-starch, soy sauce and sugar to a small bowl and stir to combine.

Heat a wok or large frying pan until hot. Add the sesame oil, garlic, ginger, and green onions and stir-fry with a spatula until fragrant. Add the black beans and Sichuan pepper and continue stir-frying.

Add the ground pork and use the spatula to break it up into small grains. When the pork is cooked, add the doubanjiang and stir to distribute. Add the tofu and toss to mix.

Give the stock mixture a good stir to incorporate anything that may have settled, and then pour it over the pork and tofu. Toss to coat, then boil until the sauce thickens.

Garnish with the chopped spring onion, chilli, then served with hot rice.

Burnt pork belly

Many people say that this is the quintessential dish of Shanghai. The meat is soft without being greasy and has origins that can be traced back to the Song Dynasty (11th-12th century). There was a great flood of water in Jiangsu province when Sodongpa (a famous poet, writer, and politician from the 11th century) was in its possession (the office to monitor the water bodies). At that time, the Soldier led the camps and the people and built the embankments to prevent the entire city from being submerged. The people sent pork as a token of gratitude for the work, and the soul was healed from eating the pork and sharing it with the people.

Serves 4-6

2 pieces of pork belly, about 180g each

4 tbsp sugar

1 tbsp vegetable oil

FOR THE SAUCE:

5 tbsp soy sauce

3 tbsp sugar

1 tbsp minced, garlic

3 dried red chillies

2 litres of water

FOR THE GARNISH:

4 bunches of pak choi

4 fresh red chillies

4 small sized pumpkins

4 tbsp chilli seeds (optional)

100g lentils

Heat a non-stick frying pan with vegetable oil before adding the sugar. Cook until caramelised and brown in colour. Pat dry the pork belly and place skin side down in the frying pan. Press down with a plate to cover, otherwise hot oil will splash everywhere. Stay away from the heat. It takes about 10 minutes to get evenly burnt. Remove from the heat.

Bring to the boil a large pot filled with the water, soy sauce, sugar, garlic and red chillies. Then add the pork and cover and simmer for 30 minutes on a medium heat.

Meanwhile in another large pot bring water to the boil and add the lentils and the pumpkin. In the same water, blanch the pak choi for just one minute before removing and plunging into cold water. Drain and set aside.

Allow the lentils and pumpkin to cook for 10-15 minutes before draining and setting aside. Mix the ingredients for the sauce.

Once the pork is cooked, take off the heat, and transfer to a serving bowl with a scoop of the soy sauce and garnish with a spoonful of the lentils, pumpkin, pak choi, seeds, and red chilli to serve.

Best served with plain warm rice.

Japan

Westerners may question why Japan has become more advanced than many other Asian countries. I think it is because Japan accepted Europe and America earlier than the rest of Asia and then developed their own way.

In the 15th century Japan accepted guns and chillies, other food from Portugal, which changed all of their following wars (these two items have also changed Korea, with whom the Japanese have had many wars over the centuries).

Oda Nobunaga was a military leader who nearly unified Japan in the 1560s. He was known as the most powerful daimyo (a great lord serving under the shogun) in Japan and was responsible for equipping the army with muskets. He quickly learned the skill of firearm manufacture, and this allowed Japan to begin producing their own guns.

Having obtained the latest weaponry from the West, the Japanese only needed an opportunity to test them out domestically and internationally and this they did in 1592 by attacking Korea. Though Oda was not successful in his dream, his successor Toyotomi Hideyoshi eventually carried his wish and united the country.

Kyoto style

Sake no Hana (Sake with flowers) with bento

If you ever visit Japan, I recommend that you skip the big cities of Tokyo and Osaka and instead visit Kyoto first. Kyoto is the old capital of Japan, known for its geisha, Kaiseki (a tasting menu selected by the chef) and its cherry blossoms. It is incredibly beautiful, surrounded by many temples, shrines, palaces and traditional gardens.

The best time to visit is in April, during the cherry blossom season. At this time, the city is covered in pink and white cherry flowers that make it so dramatically breath-taking. During this spectacular season, people walk day and night along the canals, parks and ponds, or through the forests full of weeping willows and cherry trees.

Underneath a cherry tree is the perfect place to enjoy a bento (a box containing a single portion of food) made of local specialties. A wonderful spot to stroll down the Kano River and visit Gion, the prettiest place in Kyoto, where you can say hello to Geishas and if you are lucky, take a photo with them.

Japanese food

Japan has an undoubtedly big food culture. Popular dishes there include bento sushi, udon and soba, ramen noodles, tempura, and unagi.

The Japanese love bento so much that you can find bento shops everywhere - even in vending machines at any station. I highly recommend that you pick up a Kyoto- style bento 'Ekiben' (known as a 'train station bento') or an 'upgraded version' made by a local chef, where you can taste the popular Kyoto specialities. You could even prepare your own at home for lunch!

Okinawa super Grannies - the longevity menu

Okinawa is a small island in Kyushu, southwest of Japan, nearby Taiwan.

The people of Okinawa are among the longest-lived people in the world and residents there have lower rates of cancer, heart disease and dementia than residents in other parts of the world. The average lifespan is 85 years old, and many of them are over 100!

An Okinawan's longevity can be attributed to good genes, but it's also thought that the island's moderate climate and clean diet could also be a factor.

The traditional diet is low in calories and fat but high in carbs, emphasizing vegetables and soy products. They eat less meat, fish and dairy products so are closer to a vegan diet. Food here is rich in essential vitamins and minerals, including antioxidants and always features plenty of fruit and sea vegetables; as a result, Okinawan super grannies tend to look much younger and have fewer wrinkles.

I think that we should all take the time to prepare a more vegetarian menu. Some highlights of Okinawan cuisine that you could try making or using yourself are:

Purple sweet potato
Sea vegetables kombu and wakame
Turmeric
Bitter melon
Soybeans products like tofu and miso
Buckwheat noodle
Seasoning with a light soy sauce

Edamame
Miso soup
Bitter gourd with tofu
Steamed vegetables with buck wheat noodles

Classic and back in the 16th century when adapted a foreign food.

Yellow tail sashimi
Scallop sashimi
Chirashi
Unadon
Tempura
Castella

Yellowtail sashimi

The word of sashimi can be daunting or scary for some people.
If you can get the purest and freshest fish for sashimi, it's divine! Infused with a light dressing and fresh fruits, this is definitely one to try.

Serves 4

400g yellowtail fillets
½ pear, cored, sliced, soaked in sugar water

FOR THE HERBS JUICE:
a bunch of parsley
100g spinach

FOR THE DRESSING:
3 tbsp olive oil
1 tbsp soy sauce
1 squeeze of lemon
1 tbsp mustard
salt and pepper

FOR THE GARNISH:
a few edible flowers, petals
a few dill leaves torn
10 sprigs of chives, finely chopped
½ pear julienne

To make herbs juice

Bring a pot of water to the boil with a pinch of salt and blanch the parsley and spinach for 1-2 minutes. Plunge into ice water and drain. Place the blanched herbs with 3 tbsp water into a food processor to blitz. Pass through a sieve and keep in the fridge.

To make the dressing: add the olive oil, soy sauce, mustard, lemon juice, salt, and pepper to a bowl and mix well.

Prepare the fish using a very sharp knife to slice the yellow tail into 0.5cm thick pieces. On a serving plate, draw a line across with the herb juice, then place the sashimi and sliced pear in middle. Drizzle the dressing over the sashimi and chives and add petals to garnish

Scallop sashimi

Fresh scallops: what a treasure! In any sort of cooking, they are seriously delicious. Scallops are very tender and delicate and full of flavourful sweetness.

This sashimi version includes a fancy Japanese yuzu dressing that will enhance the flavour even more.

If you live near the coast have easy access to fresh fish and seafood, make sure you take advantage! You are so lucky!

Serves 4

12-15 fresh scallops, cleaned, separate the coral

2 tbsp chives, finely chopped

3 tbsp lemon zest, soak in sugar water

fresh ginger, julienne

1 tbsp of pomelo segment

FOR THE YUZU DRESSING:

½ cup of grapeseed oil

1 tbsp soy sauce

3 tbsp yuzu juice

1 tbsp minced, garlic

3 tbsp extra-virgin olive oil

salt and pepper

Whisk the grapeseed oil, soy sauce, yuzu juice, and garlic in a medium bowl. Season the dressing to taste with the salt and pepper.

For the scallop: carefully and thinly slice it on a clean board.

Place the scallop in the middle of a serving plate and drizzle over the dressing. Garnish with the pomelo, chives, ginger, and lemon zest.

Chirashi

This dish is bold and vivid with the colour of fresh fish and vegetables. The fish, seafood, vegetables, and egg sit on a bedding of rice. It is the perfect dish for lunch.

Serves 4-6

20 prawns
100g tuna, cut into dice
100g salmon, cut into dice
100g tobiko
8 snow peas
3 eggs, beaten
1 sheet of nori, shredded
12 edamame pods, skinned
2 cups of rice
2½ cups of water

Wash the rice with cold water until the water runs clear. Drain well. If you have a rice cooker, cook the rice following the manufacturer's instruction.

Without a rice cooker, take a heavy saucepan and add the rice and cold water. Bring to the boil for 10 minutes, then turn the heat down and cook for another 5 minutes. Turn off the heat and leave for a further 5-10 minutes, letting the rice cool down a little.

To make the egg omelette:

Add the beaten eggs and fry gently for a couple of minutes on each side, until set. Leave it on a chopping board to cool, then roll over and thinly slice.

Par boil the edamame beans and the snow peas until just wilted. Remove and chill for a few minutes in cold water. Keep the boiling water for later Peel the edamame and snow peas then chop into small pieces. Using the same boiling water, cook the prawns for 3-5 minutes, then plunge into ice water. Drain, remove the head and peel the skin.

Using a sharp knife cut the salmon and tuna into chunks.

In a bowl, place the rice then arrange the salmon, tuna, prawns, tobiko, egg, snow peas, edamame beans, and nori on top.

Unadon

Unadon combines the words Unagi (freshwater eel) and Donburi (a rice-bowl dish).

Unagi is the Japanese word for freshwater eel which you may see on sushi set eel fillets that are glazed with sweetened soy-based sauce.

Japanese love unagi. There is a tradition of eating unagi on a particular mid-summer day in order to gain stamina during the hot summer. Some people are put off by picturing a sea snake, but I promise: it's very tasty. For many, unagi is one of the best foods around, so give it a try.

Serves 4

450g short grain rice
600ml water
400g unagi, skin on

FOR THE SAUCE:
4 tbsp soy sauce
2 tbsp mirin
1½ tbsp cooking sake
2½ tbsp sugar

Preheat the oven to 180°C/Gas Mark 4.

Rinse the rice several times. Add enough water to cover, plus a little extra, and bring to the boil for 10 minutes. Reduce to a medium heat for another 10 minutes then remove from the heat and leave.

To make the sauce, combine the mirin and sake in a small saucepan and bring to the boil. Reduce the heat and add the sugar, stirring until completely dissolved. Add the soy sauce and bring to the boil. Reduce the heat and simmer for 10 minutes, or until the sauce thickens. Turn off the heat and set aside to cool.

Cut the unagi to fit the size of your rice bowl.

Line a baking tray with aluminium foil. Lay the fillets on top and brush with vegetable oil. Place on the grilling unit and grill for 5-7 minutes until nicely browned.

Take the fillets out of the oven and carefully cover with the unagi sauce. Place the fillets back on the grilling unit to grill a further minute or so, until the sauce starts to bubble on top.

To serve, add cooked rice to a serving bowl, brush the top of the rice with the remaining sauce and lay the unagi fillets on top

Tempura

Who doesn't like a freshly deep-fried tempura?

The tempura is crispy, crunchy and light. The key for perfect tempura is simple if you remember 3 things:

1. Loosen up the batter

2. The ingredients and batter should be cooled

3. The oil temperature has to be 170°C

Tempura batter should prepared in a small batch using chopsticks or hands to mix for a few seconds. Don't worry about left over lumps because if over-mixed, the gluten in the wheat will activate, causing the batter to become soft when fried.

The batter and the ingredients must also be really cold before you deep fry.

To test the oil and batter are ready for frying, you should drop a small amount of batter in the frying oil; if it pops straight back up, it's ready to go. ZTempura was introduced by the Portuguese in the international port of 'Nagasaki' through the fritter cooking technique.

Serves 4-6

12 king fresh prawns, shelled

FOR THE TEMPURA DIP:

3 tbsp soy sauce
1 tbsp sake
1 tbsp mirin
1 tsp water
1 tsp grated ginger
1 tsp grated mooli

FOR THE BATTER:

1 egg yolk
200ml cup of iced water, plus more if necessary
1 cup tempura flour, plus more for dusting
a pinch of salt

FOR THE VEGETABLES:

1 eggplant
½ carrot, sliced
½ sweet potato, sliced

In a medium bowl, gently mix water, the tempura flour, one egg yolk, and a pinch of salt. It's is ok if the batter is lumpy. Place the batter in the fridge while preparing other ingredients, adding them to the fridge as you go.

Make some cuts across the shrimp belly and remove the veins. Gently flatten them using your thumb to prevent curling while frying. Make sure you press well enough to elongate them. Keep in the fridge.

On a separate plate, add the flour. Dust the prawns in the flour. Remove and dip in batter from the fridge.

Heat the oil to 170°C and drop a little of the batter mix into the oil. When it pops straight back up, it means the oil is ready to start cooking in. In a jiggling motion, get rid of excess batter on the prawns. Holding them by tail, dip in the hot oil and jiggle again before letting go. Cook until the colour changes, turning them halfway through cooking.

Repeat this jiggling method with the remaining ingredients. Place on a paper towel.

Add the grated daikon and ginger in a light soy sauce and serve with the hot tempura straight away.

Castella

Kasutera is a Japanese style castella sponge cake made with flour, sugar, eggs, and honey. This Nagasaki speciality was brought to Japan in the 16th century by the Portuguese. This old fashion recipe prepares egg whisked with sugar to a ribbon stage, which is folded with flour and baked in a wooden frame for 50 minutes. The castella should be moist, light, and with a very fine texture.

Serves 4-10

280g bread flour
40g cake flour
30g vegetable oil
30g honey
30g corn syrup
20g rum
20g mirin
60ml milk
14 egg yolk
110g sugar

FOR THE MERINGUE:
12 egg whites
230g sugar
3g salt
3g vanilla extract

Preheat oven to 200°C/Gas Mark 6.

Mix the bread flour and the cake flour together. Then pass through a sieve and double sift the flour. Set aside.

In a mixing bowl, whisk the honey, vegetable oil, corn syrup, rum, mirin, and milk together (you can briefly heat in the microwave if you are unable to mix). Set aside.

Using an electric mixer, beat the egg yolk slowly at first until they Break down and begin to get a bit sticky. Whisk for about 3-5 minutes until the mixture turns in colour, reaching what's called the ribbon stage which refers to the thick, pale, foam. Add the liquid mixture into the egg batter. Remove from the bowl and set aside.

To make meringue:

Using an electric mixer, whisk the egg white and the salt until soft peaks form. Gradually add the sugar, a tablespoon at a time, whisking until the sugar dissolves. Once all the sugar has been added, continue to whisk on high for 3 minutes, then whisk in the vanilla extract. The meringue should be stiff and glossy.

Slowly add small amounts of the meringue to the egg yolk mix and one third of the sifted flour. Fold it in gently until the flour is just combined. Repeat with the remaining meringue and flour. Do not over mix. When you see lumps just rub gently with a spatula.

Put some parchment paper in a baking tin and pour the batter into it. Using a skewer, draw a zigzag line to remove any large air bubbles from the batter. This will give an even texture throughout the finished cake.

Bake at 180°C in a preheated oven for 25 minutes until the top turns a rich brown. Then quickly cover it with parchment paper and lower the temperature to 170°C and continue baking for another 25 minutes. It will take about 50 minutes in total. Test with a skewer: when it comes out clean the cake is done.

When done, turn the cake over onto a flat plate. While it is still hot, put it in a plastic bag and leave it for 12 hours so that the cake will have a moist texture. Before serving, slice off the sides of the cake.

Edamame

Edamame is the soft and edible form of an immature soybean.

Green pods are boiled or steam and served with salt. Edamame beans are naturally gluten free and low in calories, contain no cholesterol and they are an excellent source of protein, iron and calcium. Edamame is a popular dish outside of Japan.

Serves 4-8

1 pack of frozen edamame

3 tsp sea salt

Parboil the edamame, drain, toss with the sea salt. Serve.

Miso soup

Miso is a fermented soybean paste. It's well known for soups, stews, dressings, or marinades. Miso is used lots of different ways, not only Japan but also across Asian cuisine.

Miso soup is very easy to make as well as being a popular dish.

It's so warm and comforting, served with sliced tofu, and seaweed; chopped spring onion enhances the flavour and adds nutrients, too.

The dish as a whole is incredibly nutritious and linked to a variety of health benefits, including better digestion and a stronger immune system.

Serves 4-6

FOR THE DASHI (STOCK):

30g dried kombu

3 shiitake mushrooms, soak in warm water, chopped

½ mooli, peeled, thinly sliced

6 cups of water

¼ cup miso

1 pack of silken tofu, drained and cut into 2 x 2cm cubes

½ cup of dried wakame seaweed,

soaked in warm water, chopped

3 tbsp spring onion, thinly sliced

a pinch of salt

Make the dashi

Bring the water and the mooli, shiitake mushroom, and kombu to a boil in a large saucepan and cook for about 10 minutes. Remove the kombu. Continue to boil the remaining ingredients for another 10 minutes then remove from the heat. Pass through a sieve or into a bowl.

Stir together the miso and ½ cup of the prepared dashi stock in a saucepan until smooth. Add the remaining dashi and heat. Once hot, gently stir in the tofu and wakame. Simmer for 1 minute and remove from the heat. Season with salt and serve.

Bitter gourd stuffed with tofu

Bitter gourd is a humble vegetable, not well-known in the West. It is surprisingly good for your body and can be treated as a medicine.

If you eat bitter gourd by itself, it can be too bitter, but stuffed with seasoned tofu it is very tasty, and good for your health. As a rich source of antioxidants, it helps reduce your risks for a number of health issues, including fighting off inflammation, diabetes management, and playing a role in the lowering of blood sugar and cholesterol levels.

Serves 4

2 bitter gourds
180g firm tofu
2 dried wood ear mushrooms (black fungus)
salt and pepper
100g black sesame seeds
3 tbsp sesame oil
a pinch of salt

Soak the mushrooms in warm water for 20 minutes. Drain and squeeze out any excess water. Remove the stems and cut the caps into thin strips.

Cut the gourds into 3cm rounds slices. Hollow out using a teaspoon and discard the seeds.

Place the tofu on a chopping board and using the back of a knife smear the tofu to make an sort of puree.

Put the mushrooms, tofu, salt, and pepper and in a bowl. Mix until the tofu is smooth and creamy. Spoon the mixture into the gourd slices, then steam for 15 minutes, or until they are tender when pierced with a skewer.

Combine the black sesame seeds into a blender and blitz until they become a powder. Slowly add the sesame oil, mixing until a smooth puree and season with a pinch of salt. Use a spoonful of the sesame puree to draw on the serving plate and add the cooked bitter gourds.

Steamed vegetables with buckwheat noodles

Roast vegetables are very common in European cuisine, but Asians tend to eat steamed or lightly blanched vegetables, tossing them with a light sauce or serving them with dips. The main idea is to try not to lose nutrients by overcooking and enjoying a lighter version of these vegetables.

Serves 4

a small bunch of asparagus, trimmed

a small bunch broccoli

1 pack pak choi, broken leaves

1 large purple sweet potato

1 large sweet potato

4 okras

1 large bitter gourd, seeded, sliced

a small lotus root, peeled and soaked in 1 tbsp vinegar with water

½ silken tofu (about 100g), broken

100g buckwheat noodles

a pinch of salt

FOR THE SEASONED MISO:

2 tbsp miso

1 tbsp soy sauce

1 tbsp sugar

2 tbsp water

1 tbsp sesame oil

FOR THE BLACK SESAME PUREE:

100g black sesame

3 tbsp sesame oil

a pinch of salt

Place the sweet potato and purple potato into a steam pot to cook For about 15 minutes, then remove. Set aside.

Bring a large saucepan of water to the boil and blanch in the following order: first the beansprout, followed by asparagus, okra, broccoli, pak choi, bitter gourd, and finally the lotus root. Plunge each into iced water and drain.

Meanwhile in another saucepan with a boiling water, blanch the tofu for 1-2 minutes. Cook the noodles for 5 minutes then plunge into ice water, drain and set aside.

In a mixing bowl, add the miso, sugar, soy, water, and sesame oil and mix well. Transfer into a serving bowl.

Place the black sesame seed into a food processor then blitz for about 1 minute until it becomes a powder. Next, add the oil and blitz again until it becomes puree. Season with salt. Transfer onto a serving plate, making a circle in a middle of the plate. Arrange the blanched vegetables and noodles. Serve with the miso dip.

Korea

I am proud to be Korean as we have an incredible heritage. Food in Korea is typified by an array of dishes. At least 10 to 15 small plates called 'banchan' including rice, soup, meat, fish, kimchi, and other side dishes are all served together in one meal (a little like Spanish tapas). For me, this is the closest to a perfect meal you can get, with an ideal nutritional balance. This meal, called a 'Bapssang', is the best way to eat a lot of vegetables in one meal. Korean people eat a lot, but somehow we stay slim.

Korean heroes of war and food

Kimchi is one of Korea's best-known foods and it has a long history. For a long time, Kimchi was white and more akin to normal pickles, but in the 16th century, during a period of war with Japan, chillies were introduced to Korea via the Portuguese links with Japan. At that time, chilli wasn't thought to be useful for cooking and Was instead used a weapon to attack the enemy's eyes (like pepper spray). But in the 18th century, Korea began using it for Kimchi and other foods and now chilli is an essential ingredient in Korean cooking.

In the 16th century, Korea underwent many important events such as the appearance of a national hero and the culinary evolution.

Admiral Yi Sun-Shin became a national hero in Korea for his prowess in battle. He fought 23 naval battles with Japan and won every single one of them. He must have been a terrifying figure to the Japanese soldiers. It was said that if they saw Admiral Yi Sun-Shin at sea, they must run. To run was to save a life.

Yi Sun-Shin's ship was shaped like a turtle, with the main body covered by metal that spread out like a roof over its top deck, protecting the men inside. The hull of the ship was fitted with a small window through which the sailors could fire cannons or arrows – like a precursor to modern battleship. It must have been a terrifying sight.

In 1597, Yi Sun-Shin won his most famous victory at the Battle of Myeong-Nyang. He commanded a meagre 13 ships against 333 Japanese ships. Japanese soldiers were well-trained and had many experiences in war, meaning they could have easily won in a face-to -face battle. At the time, Korea hadn't been at war for nearly 200 years, the nation was in peace, making Japan's invasion so shocking. Amazingly, he defeated the Japanese and (more amazingly considering his fearsome reputation) let them go home.

He was self-supported, taking care of refugees and soldiers by farming and catching fish without support from a central government. And despite his astonishing victories, he wasn't trained as a naval commander. However, thanks to his determination and ingenuity, he is thought of as one of the greatest naval commanders in history.

Korean food

As I explained earlier, Koreans eat a lot at tables bursting with food and, though there are many varieties, it is very simple cooking which is respectful of ancient cooking methods. Food is cooked by braising, boiling, or blanching before tossing it with sauces. These sauces are commonly made with soy, garlic, ginger, spicy chilli powder, sugar, and fish sauce with soybean pastes (like denjang, gochujang) for seasoning.

Koreans eat lots of vegetables with their meat and fish, both raw or parboiled, and tossed with a light sauce.

Janchi'a festival menu:

Beef tartare
Cold noodles
Spring Onion Pancake
Assorted meat, mushroom, dumpling in light broth
Slow cooked beef stew braised short ribs

Tiger Mum's bapssang:

Rice cake
Braised mackerel with kimchi, mooli and potato
Spinach
Egg roll with seaweed
Dried anchovy
Deodeok
Braised spice tofu
Rice

Beef tartare

Chilled beef tartare, seasoned with soy, garlic, sesame oil and sugar. The tender meat almost melts in your mouth. This is kind of dish never fails to bring a smile. And it's so simple to make.

Serves 4

100g beef fillet, chilled in the freezer for 30 minutes

1 tbsp soy sauce

1 tbsp sugar

½ tsp sesame oil

1 tbsp minced garlic

FOR THE GARNISH:

4 egg yolks

½ Korean pear or William pear

a pinch of pepper

a pinch of turmeric

a bunch of spinach leaves

a handful of edible flowers or petals

2 tbsp gochujang (Korean chilli paste)

1 tbsp lemon juice

Chill the beef in the freezer for 30 minutes, then thinly slice the beef.

Combine all ingredients, the soy sauce, sugar, sesame oil and garlic with the beef in a bowl.

Peel, and core the pear, then cut into julienne and sprinkle lemon juice over the pear.

This is a time to harness your creativity and be an artist with your presentation. Line up white round plates, take a spoonful of Gochujang paste on a spatula or back of a spoon, and smear the paste on the plates any way you like. Don't be nervous, just do it your way!

On one edge of the plate place the marinated beef, and on the other side set the pear slices. Carefully place the egg yolk on to the plate.

Dust on a pinch of turmeric powder over the egg yolk and garnish the plate with the spinach leaves and edible flowers. Before you eat mix the beef tartare with the egg yolk - it will be much softer.

Cold noodles

Perfect for a hot sizzling summer's day. Originally from North Korean, it is now a very popular dish throughout Korea. A few years ago, North and South leaders met for peace talks. That day people would eat cold noodles as a wish for peace and hope in both countries. This dish is cooling with subtle flavours.

Serves 4

100g rump steak

400g cold noodles, (naeng myeon) or soba noodles

4 cups of beef stock

2 hardboiled eggs, peeled, cut into half

1 egg, beaten and seasoned with a pinch of salt

1 tbsp oil

1 cucumber, sliced into 12 pieces

1 pear

1 tbsp soy sauce

3 tbsp vinegar

Place the beef in a large pan with beef stock. Bring to the boil and simmer for 10 minutes until the beef is cooked through. Remove the heat and keep it refrigerated. Once cool, thinly slice.

In a bowl, combine the beef stock season with soy sauce and vinegar. Keep it refrigerated until cool.

In a frying pan add oil and place over a medium heat. Pour the beaten egg and fry gently for 1-2 minutes, cooking both sides. Remove from the pan and cool, then cut into julienne.

Put the noodles into the large pan, cover with boiling salted water and cook until just cooked through. Plunge into cold water then drain. Peel and core the pear and slice.

Divide the noodles into serving bowls, place the sliced meat, cucumber, pear, and egg omelette, with half a boiled egg to garnish. Pour over the chilled stock.

Spring onion pancake

In Korea, we eat pancakes on rainy days with rice sake. It's a simple batter with vegetables and seafood. Deliciously crispy, it is just so good!

Serves 2-4

2 tbsp glutinous rice flour
100g plain flour
1 tsp salt
cup of water
3-4 spring onions, cut into 5cm length
3 tiger prawns, washed, peeled, and deveined
1 squid, roughly chopped
½ carrot, cut into julienne
½ courgette, cut into julienne
½ yellow pepper, seeded, thinly sliced
a small bunch of chives, cut into 5cm lengths

FOR THE DIPS:

3 tbsp soy sauce
1tsp sugar
1 tsp vinegar
1 tbsp chopped spring onion
a pinch of sesame seed
1 tsp chopped chilli
a few coriander leaves

Combine the flour and salt with the water to make a smooth, reasonably thin batter. Mix with the spring onion, prawns, squid, carrot, courgette, and yellow pepper and set aside.

To make the dip, put the the soy sauce, sugar, vinegar in a mixing bowl and whisk well before adding the remaining ingredients. Pour into a dipping bowl.

Heat 2 tbsp of the oil in a non-stick frying pan and when moderately hot, add a small ladleful of the batter, spreading to make a thin pancake.

Cook until golden brown underneath and starting to set on top - about 2 minutes - then turn over and cook until light brown on the other side. Repeat until all the mixture is used up. Cut into 8 pieces and garnish with the chives.

Serve hot with the soy and vinegar dip.

Assorted meat, mushroom, dumpling in light broth

This celebrated dish is known as trader's food. The story goes that when two traders couldn't reach a proper price, haggling and arguing, one trader invited the other to share this dish as an offer of generosity. Finally, after the meal had been shared, a deal was made. A happy ending for the traders!

Serves 4-6

1 kg brisket beef stock
1 onion, chopped
3 garlic cloves
3 spring onions

FOR THE SEASONING:

1 tbsp minced garlic
3 tbsp soy sauce
a pinch of salt and pepper

FOR THE DUMPLINGS:

50g minced beef
1 tbsp soy sauce
1 tsp sesame oil
a pinch of salt and pepper
1 tbsp chopped spring onion
3 tbsp squeezed tofu-optional
2 tbsp chopped cabbage
1 pack of dumpling wrappers

FOR THE GARNISH:

90g sweet potato noodle
3 boiled eggs, halves
1 pack enoki mushroom
1 pack king oyster mushroom
5 perilla leaves-optional can use rocket

FOR THE DIPS:

3 tbsp soy sauce
1 tsp sugar
1 tbsp water
a pinch of chilli flakes
a pinch of sesame seeds
1 tsp spring onion, chopped

Put the brisket, the onion, garlic, and spring onion in a large pot and cover with 3 litres of cold water. Bring to the boil for 20 minutes then simmer for 2 hours with the lid off. Remove any dark foam.

Strain the stock, seasoning it with the minced garlic, soy sauce, salt and pepper. Slice the meat. Boil the eggs for 7-10 minutes, cool and peel.

To make the dumplings, combine all the ingredients for the dumpling fillings in a bowl.

Lay out the dumpling wrappers on a clean kitchen surface and place one spoonful of the dumpling filling into the centre of each wrapper. Use a pastry brush to lightly moisten the edges of the wrapper with water, then fold the wrapper and firmly press the edges closed.

Bring the stock back to the boil. Add the dumplings and the sliced meat and simmer for 10 minutes. Finish by adding the mushroom and noodles for another 5 minutes.

Arrange the meat, dumplings, noodles, cooked eggs, and mushroom in a large bowl. Place the dipping sauce in the middle and garnish with the greens.

Rice cake

A traditional Korean dessert. When it comes to celebrating, we serve this dish on any occasions, whether for weddings, birthdays, the New Year, or lunar festival. We also share this dish with new neighbours when they move to new a house. Deliciously made with rice flour and a little sugar, it is even better with a lot of nuts, seeds, and fragrant spices.

Serves 4-6

1 tbsp cinnamon powder
1 tbsp paprika
1 tbsp pistachio chopped
1 tbsp pine nuts chopped
1 tbsp peanuts chopped
1 tbsp sesame seeds
1 tbsp black sesame seeds
1 tbsp brown sugar
10g rice noodles, deep fried
1 cup of sticky rice flour
3 tbsp warm water

FOR THE FILLINGS:

½ cup of red beans, soaked overnight
10 dates, stoned and finely chopped
3 tbsp sugar
1 tsp cinnamon powder
a pinch of salt

Place the beans in a pan, cover with water and bring to the boil for 20 minutes until the beans are cooked. Then drain.

Roll them between the palms of your hands to make a puree.

Simmer the puree in a pan until the paste is smooth then add the sugar and toss in the dates, cinnamon, and season with a pinch of salt.

Sift the flour and the salt into a bowl and add warm water. Mix well and knead for 10 minutes. Take a small piece of dough, make an indent with your finger and add a little bean paste. Wrap the dough over and make into a ball.

Bring a large pan of water to the boil and add the rice balls. Cook for 5 minutes, then drain.

Sprinkling some of the spice powder on a plate, roll the rice balls to achieve a light coating.

To serve, plate the spice and nut powders with the sesame seeds using a fork to move them around. Get creative! Place the rice cake on the plate and garnish with the fried noodles.

Slow cooked beef stew braised short ribs

This recipe is always in top demand from my customers.
Slow cooked beef with a delicious blend of spices, fruit, and vegetables leaves it mouth-watering and tender.
To get the best ribs, visit a local butcher and order them in advance, asking for them to be cut to size.

Serves 4-6

1kg beef ribs, cut in 2½cm pieces
1 apple, peeled, cored
1 pear, peeled, cored
½ onion roughly chopped
3 spring onions, roughly chopped

FOR THE GARNISH:

1 bunch kai lan Chinese green
a small bunch of beansprouts

FOR THE SAUCE:

⅓ cup (85ml) light soy sauce
2½ tbsp rice wine
2½ tbsp sesame oil
2 tbsp sugar
6-8 cloves of garlic, minced
2 spring onions, finely chopped
freshly ground pepper to taste

Rinse the beef ribs in cold water, then drain. Blanch in boiling water for 10 minutes.

Place the apple, pear, onion, spring onion into a blender and blitz until it becomes a puree.

For the sauce: whisk together the soy sauce, rice wine, sesame oil, sugar, minced garlic, spring onion, and ground pepper in a bowl. Marinate the meat with the blended fruit for 1 hour, then transfer to a saucepan. Add water to cover the ribs. Bring to a boil for 20 minutes on a high heat and cover with a lid. Turn to a lower heat and gently simmer for about 2 hours until the meat is tender.

Put the beansprouts and kai lan in a pan with the salt and add boiling water. Blanch the beanssprout and kai lan for a few seconds before plunging them into cold water and draining.

Scoop the ribs into a serving bowl and pour a spoonful of sauce over the meat, then garnish with the kai lan and bean sprouts. Serve hot.

Braised mackerel with kimchi, mooli and potato

Meaty mackerel - eaten with braised kimchi, mooli, and potato - absorbs all the spices and is incredibly delicious. Mackerel is a very popular fish year-round. It is reasonably cheap and cooked with aged kimchi and vegetables, it is perfect for a winter diet.

Serves 4

2 large mackerels, chopped into 4-5 pieces
100g aged kimchi, chopped
100g mooli, peeled
4 potatoes, peeled, cut into half
1 tsp vegetable oil

FOR THE SAUCE:
120ml soy sauce
2 tbsp sake or white wine
2 tbsp honey
3 garlic cloves, crushed
2 tsp chilli powder
½ onion, chopped
1 red chilli, chopped
1 green chilli, chopped
1 tbsp denjang (Korean beans paste)

Slice the mackerel into medium size pieces. If the fish is big, cut into 3 pieces, if it's small, cut into 2. Use a very sharp knife.

Cut the mooli into slices. Add kimchi and a drizzle of 1 tbsp vegetable oil into a large pan, arranging it evenly across the base. Cover with a layer of mooli and potato and top with a layer of mackerel.

In a bowl, add the soy sauce, sake, honey, garlic, denjang, chilli powder, onion, and chillies. Mix well then pour over the fish and cover the pan with a lid.

Place over a high heat and bring the liquid to boil for 5 minutes then reduce the heat and simmer for 8-10 minutes or until the fish is tender. Spoon the liquid over the fish as it cooks. Ladle into bowls and serve immediately.

Spinach

This is a quick dish, but very tasty and healthy. It is a great source of calcium and other nutrients, and is very easy to make.

A quick blanch of the spinach, a touch of soy sauce, garlic, sesame oil, spring onion, and seasoned with a bit of salt and tossed with sesame seeds, this could not bet easier.

Korean spinach is different from the UK. It's much smaller in size, and instead of eating just baby spinach, they eat the whole thing. It is so flavoursome and sweet.

Serves 4-6

a bunch about 300g spinach with stems, washed and drained blanched in boiling water for 30 seconds, chopped

1 tsp sesame seeds, toasted and coarsely crushed while still warm

1 tsp sesame oil

2 tbsp soy sauce

½ tsp salt

1 tbsp minced garlic

In a bowl, toss the spinach with the salt then add the soy sauce, garlic, a drizzle of sesame oil, sesame seeds, and serve.

Dried Anchovy

Crispy anchovies in soy sauce with goji berry and sesame seeds. Such great variety in one dish, and highly nutritious!

Serves 4-6

½ cup dried small anchovies

2 tbsp soy sauce

1 tbsp sugar

½ tsp Korean sesame oil

½ tsp sesame seeds

1 tbsp goji berry

1 tbsp mixed seeds

1 tbsp oil

Put the oil in a pan, add the anchovies and mix well. Cook for about 5 minutes until the anchovies get crispy. Add the soy sauce, sugar and stir fry for 1 minute, ensuring the ingredients are mixed together evenly. Keep mixing and tossing.

Stir in the sesame oil and seeds and remove from the heat then Toss with the mixed seeds, and goji berries. Serve at room temperature.

Egg roll with seaweed

Softly cooked egg omelette with seaweed sheets. Commonly known as 'nori', these seaweed sheets are called 'kim' in Korea.

Serves 4-6

3 medium sized eggs

1 seaweed sheet

1 tbsp oil

1 pinch of salt

Heat a pan with the oil and pour in half of the egg mix. Stir and when it starts bubbling place on the seaweed sheet and fold about 10cm from the edge. Keep folding to the end of pan, pour in the rest of the mixture, then fold over. Cool. Then slice and serve.

Deodeok

Deodeok (Condonopsis tanceolate) is known as 'meat from the mountains'. These roots are full of nutrients, including Saponin and are also known as the 'cousin of Ginseng'. It is a key medical ingredient that promotes blood circulation, energizes the body, and strengthens the respiratory system.

You can find deodeok in most Korean supermarkets.

Serves 2-4

100g deodeok, peeled

1 tbsp gochu-jang (Korean chilli paste)

1 tbs gochu-garu (Korean chilli powder)

1 tbsp soy sauce

1 tbsp sugar

1 tbsp rice syrup

1 tsp sesame seeds

1 tsp white pepper

½ tbsp minced garlic

½ tbsp minced spring onion

1 tbsp cooking wine

1 tbsp vinegar

In a mixing bowl add the gochu-jang, gochu-garu, soy sauce, sugar, and syrup. Mix well then add the garlic, spring onion, wine, and vinegar. Whisk well until all ingredients cooperate.

On a clean chopping board using a rolling pin to roll over the deodeok and break its skin, then shred. Add it to the sauce, tossing well, and add the sesame seeds, and oil to serve.

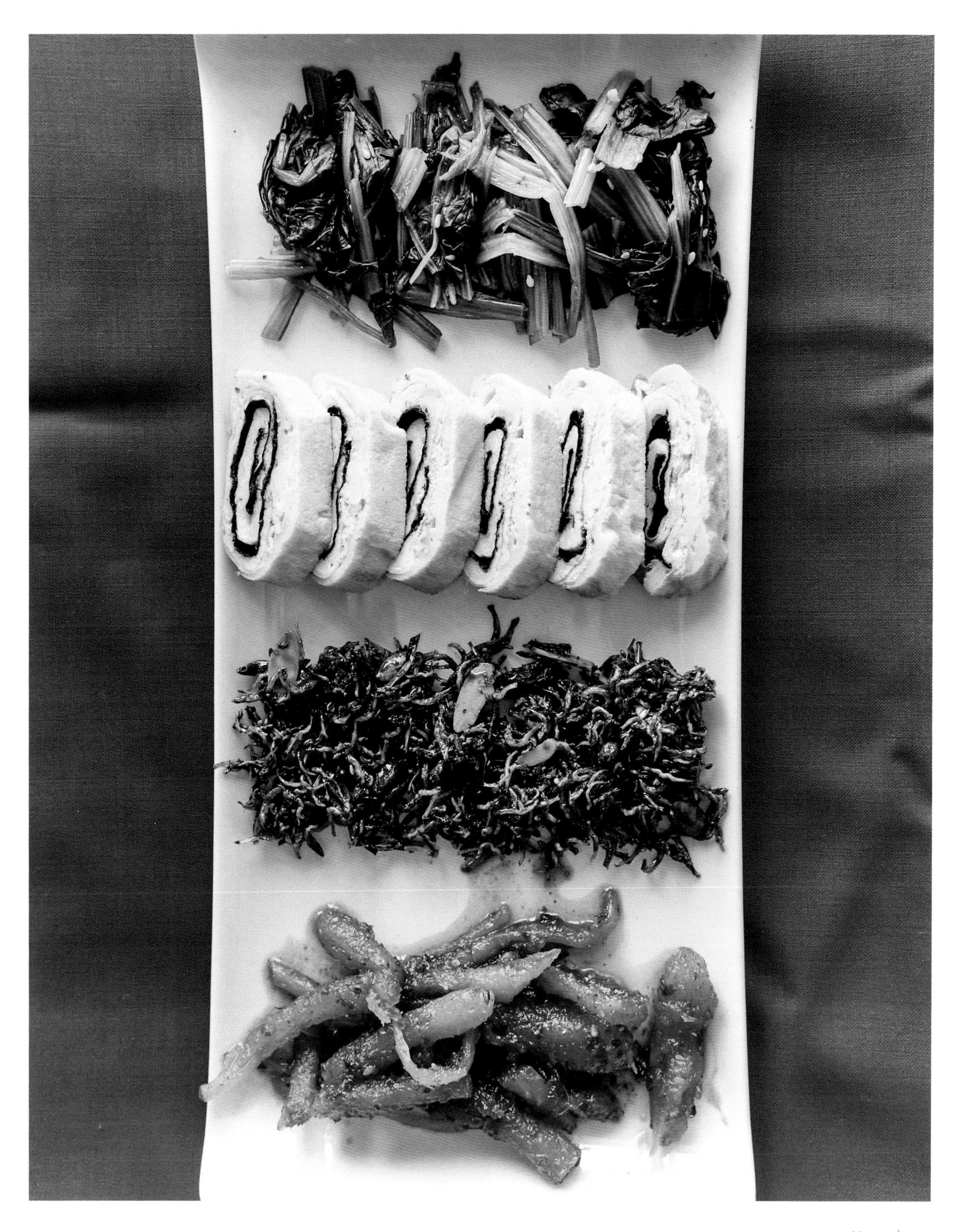

Braised spicy tofu

What a clever invention tofu is.
It is not only nutritious as a meat substitute but also lends itself to various other uses. Korean style, fried tofu slices can be seasoned with hot chilli, garlic, among other things, to transform an essentially bland food into one with distinctive flavours and a chewy texture.

Serves 4-6

3 firm tofu squares, sliced 10 x 10cm
3 tbsp vegetable oil
3 tbsp soy sauce
3 tbsp anchovy stock, substitute any stock or water
2 tsp hot red chilli powder (gochugaru)
1 tsp salt
1 tsp garlic, minced

FOR THE GARNISH
1 spring onion, chopped
chives, cut into 10cm strips
1 tsp black seasame seeds
¼ cucumber, seeded, sliced
a small bunch of rocket salad

Dry the tofu slices on paper towel, then very lightly sprinkle a few grains of salt on one side of each slice. Let stand for 10 minutes. Heat the oil in a pan and cook the tofu over moderate heat for about 3 minutes on each side. Drain on paper towels.

Mix the soy sauce, the stock (or water), chilli powder, sesame seeds, salt, garlic, and a few spring onions together in a bowl. Put 1 tablespoon of the sauce on the bottom of a pan. Cover this with the tofu slices, sprinkle with more sauce and several red chilli threads. Add another layer of tofu, more threads, and sauce and continue until all the tofu and sauce is used. Spread a few more chilli threads on the top. Rinse the sauce bowl with 2 tablespoons of water and pour it over the tofu.

Bring the liquid to a boil, cover the pan, and simmer over a low heat for 15 minutes to steam through the tofu slices. Most of the liquid will evaporate.

Garnish and serve warm with rice and salads for a vegetarian meal or with meat and fish if you prefer.

Rice

Korea and the Far East countries, including China and Japan, most often eat a short grain rice. Asian people have a love affair with rice; we eat it almost all the time. Much like bread for Westerners, we can sometimes eat rice 3 times a day. Fluffy, sweet, and warm, we can't resist.

My mum used to cook rice with many ingredients, like beans, sweet potato, aubergine, various grains, and more, to transform simple rice into a healthier version.

With mum's recipe, I remember she would pick a host of ingredients right from garden to add on to the rice.

Nowadays, you don't need to worry about how to cook rice because we have the magic rice cooker that gives perfect rice every time. It is an essential appliance in every house.

Serves 4

1 cup of rice, well rinsed in cold water, drained

1 tbsp black sticky rice

1 cup of water

3 tbsp borlotti beans

Wash the rice thoroughly in cold water, draining and repeating the action a number of times. At first the water will be very cloudy but after washing for 3-4 minutes it will start to clear. After draining, leave for a minimum of 30 minutes before cooking. The rice will absorb the moisture and when it cooked will be softer and fluffy.

If you do not have a rice cooker, then use a heavy bottomed saucepan with a tight-fitting lid. Put the rice and the beans in the pan and add water until there is slightly more water than rice. Do not salt.

Heat the rice and just as it comes to the boil put on the lid and turn the heat down low. Simmer for 15 minutes then switch off the heat and leave covered for a further 10 minutes before serving.

Spices

I would like to introduce you to some spice mixtures and sauces that you simply must have in the kitchen. They are basic, but if you know and use them, your cooking level will increase. They are easy to cook with and can be used every day to create delicious foods.

Tomato sauce

Sautéed chopped onion, add tomato puree, one spoonful of Korean chilli paste, minced garlic, a teaspoon of sugar, toasted cumin, oregano, and salt and pepper to season. When finished, top with a bunch of herbs and cheese.

Bulgogi sauce

Soy sauce, sugar, minced garlic, spring onion, pepper, sesame oil, toasted sesame seeds, rice or white wine vinegar, with grated apple, pineapple, pear and onion.

Spicy sauce

Soy sauce, chilli powder, chilli paste, garlic, shrimp paste, sugar and sesame oil.

Basic kimchi base

Chilli powder, shrimp paste, sugar, garlic, ginger, spring onion, a bit of fish stock is optional.

Garam masala

Cumin, coriander, cardamom, cloves, cinnamon and nutmeg.

Madras curry

Turmeric, coriander, cumin, fenugreek, cinnamon, cardamom, black pepper, Kashmiri chillies and curry leaves.

Zaatar – a Middle Eastern spice blend

Thyme, oregano, coriander, sesame seeds, sumac, chilli and salt.

Ras el Hanout - an earthy Moroccan style spice blend

Turmeric, cloves, aniseeds, nigella seeds, allspice seeds, cardamon, ginger, coriander, mace, cinnamon, dried mint chilli, lavender and rosebud.

Thai red chilli paste

Red bird's eye chillies, galangal, lemongrass, coriander roots, wild ginger, red shallot, garlic and shrimp paste.

When I first tried Indian curry, I found it too spicy. I grew up with spicy chillies in most meals, but the Indian curry was dryer and heavier, quite different from the spices I had ever tasted. That was 25 years ago, and my stupid attitude changed once I visited a spice plantation in Kerala. I realised how wonderful all these flavours were. God created great ingredients like cardamom, cloves, mace, nutmeg, tapioca, and pepper. I touched, smelled, picked and cooked with all of them. They weren't dry when they weren't stuck in the kitchen cupboard for years.

It was full of fragrant ingredients like cloves. I knew once they dried they were hard, but fresh ones oozed with oil and aroma when I squeezed them with my fingers.

Mace was a sexy red cover for the nutmeg. The shell was very hard, to carefully protect the nutmeg seeds inside. Cardamom and pepper were both bushes. The cardamom plant was smallish, but the pepper plant was big and tall. Knowing how to use spices is a key point that will improve your cooking.

Dried spices are better toasted on a pan to release their fragrance and improve their taste. Try it at home, and do not be afraid of using spices. Your cooking will be much better.

Index

Wizzy's Bapssang

Published by Wizzy Chung 2021

Art Direction and Layout by Steve Hughes - Adhesive Design - adhesive-design.co.uk

Published by Taylor Brothers Bristol Ltd, Units 5/6 Avon Valley Business Park, Chapel Way, Bristol BS4 4EU

ISBN: 978-1-7398666-6-2

A catalogue record for this book is available from the British Library.

Printed and bound in UK